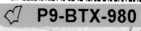

Presented by

Rev. Smith

CURRENT PROBLEMS

General Editor:
SIR ERNEST BARKER, LITT.D.

RELIGIOUS LIBERTY
TO-DAY

31

CURRENT PROBLEMS

General Editor: SIR ERNEST BARKER

RELIGIOUS LIBERTY
TO-DAY

BY

H. G. WOOD

Herbert George

CAMBRIDGE
AT THE UNIVERSITY PRESS
1949

PUBLISHED BY
THE SYNDICS OF THE CAMBRIDGE UNIVERSITY PRESS

London Office: Bentley House, N.W. 1
American Branch: New York

Agents for Canada, India, and Pakistan: Macmillan

Printed in Great Britain at the University Press, Cambridge
(Brooke Crutchley, University Printer)

CONTENTS

Chapter V, page 65

The failure of left-wing intellectuals   *page* 65

Chapter VI, page 86

The responsibilities of the Christian Church *page* 86

Chapter VII, page 110

Religious liberty in non-Christian countries—Dangers and safeguards   *page* 110

PREFATORY NOTE

THIS little book was undertaken at the suggestion of Sir Ernest Barker and the Joint Committee on Religious Liberty of which he was formerly Chairman. Without their encouragement and assistance it would never have appeared. Much of the information contained in the closing chapters has been supplied to me by the secretaries of the Committee, past and present.

In Chapter IV, I have drawn freely on the *Œcumenical Bulletin* published by the World Council of Churches. I have not given detailed references, but the quotations are taken from the issues for the current year. In Chapter V, I have made use of the greater part of an article on G. Bernard Shaw, which appeared in the *Contemporary Review* for 1934, and I am grateful for the courtesy of the Editors in agreeing to my reprint of it.

I alone am responsible for the judgements expressed in the pages that follow. I hope they will at least serve to secure further publicity for the cause with which the Joint Committee is concerned. I am much indebted to them for permission to print as an appendix their admirable statement on 'Human Rights and Religious Freedom'.

H. G. WOOD

Bournville
10 *March* 1949

CHAPTER I

RELIGIOUS LIBERTY: ITS NATURE AND SCOPE

WHEN Mill published his *Essay on Liberty* in 1859, he could point to the development and practice of religious toleration especially among the Anglo-Saxon peoples as the only effective embodiment of the broad principle of freedom of thought, discussion and conduct for which he was contending. He points out that reformers and advanced thinkers have more often questioned particular opinions and standards of conduct, held and imposed by majorities or by governing classes, than challenged the right of society to impose *any* opinions or standards.

The only case in which the higher ground has been taken on principle and maintained with consistency, by any but an individual here and there, is that of religious belief: a case instructive in many ways and not least so as forming a most striking instance of the fallibility of what is called the moral sense: for the *odium theologicum*, in a sincere bigot, is one of the most unequivocal cases of moral feeling.[1]

---

[1] *On Liberty*, pp. 6, 7 (Blackwell, 1946). Mill's allusion to moral sense refers to the controversy between Intuitionists and Utilitarians in ethics, which Lecky discusses at length in the preface to his *History of European Morals*. If Mill suggests here that to believe moral judgements to be intuitive means asserting that the truth of moral judgements may be measured by the strength of the feeling they arouse, he misunderstood the Intuitionists.

Religious minorities, which could not hope to become majorities, had to claim, and religious majorities, which could not hope to suppress minorities, had to grant toleration. So great writers asserted the great principle of religious liberty, though it 'has hardly anywhere been practically realized, except where religious indifference, which dislikes to have its peace disturbed by theological quarrels, has added its weight to the scale'. Among us in Great Britain, toleration has come to be taken more or less for granted, and religious liberty has carried with it the greater part of our civil and political liberties. When he wrote, Mill was most apprehensive of social pressures infringing individual liberty and less concerned with the possibility of the revival of legal restrictions. The influence of this essay counted for much in relaxing the social pressures whose growth he anticipated and feared. But when we survey the international scene and realize our involvement in it, the future of the tradition of toleration on which Britain prides herself may well seem doubtful, and there is a clear call for that eternal vigilance on which the defence of freedom depends. It is also clear that for such defence it will not suffice to appeal to old traditions. We must go back to first principles and reaffirm them with fresh insight and conviction.

The demand for religious liberty raises many issues. It is primarily a demand on the State to secure to the individual citizen and to organized religious groups certain rights. In a genuinely democratic State, the government is asked to protect the responsible adult citizen in holding and professing whatever ultimate beliefs commend themselves to his conscience and reason. He should be at liberty to change his beliefs if his convictions alter, and so far as government can effect it, he should not be placed at any social, economic or political disadvantage because of such change of belief. His religious liberty is infringed if government either compels or forbids him to join a particular religious association. In a fully tolerant State, the individual citizen would not be asked to carry out public duties which he could not conscientiously undertake. Particular relationships and particular callings involve additional demands. Parents cannot rightly be asked to disinterest themselves in the education, particularly in the religious education of their children. The State should respect and defend the moral and intellectual integrity of all workers, particularly of all professional workers. The maintenance of religious liberty is of especial importance to all the great professions.

Mill's essay was concerned almost exclusively with the liberty of individuals, but we have also to consider the relation of the State to religious groups and associations. The way the demand for religious liberty is interpreted and handled determines the relation of Church and State in the modern world. And since religious liberty is not a simple single right but a complex of rights, the liberty accorded by the State may be far short of the full liberty for which the Church asks.

In the four freedoms, President Roosevelt defined religious liberty as 'freedom of worship'. Clearly 'freedom of worship' may be variously interpreted. In his book *Religious Equality in Modern England* Mr Addison understands it as necessarily involving the other freedoms—freedom of speech, freedom from fear, and freedom from want. The President when he included freedom of worship in the four essential freedoms was not just paying a compliment to religion or offering a sop to the pious.

On the contrary it is arguable in logic and demonstrable in history that *freedom of worship* implies the other three: to achieve it is to achieve freedom of speech and freedom from want and fear. By freedom of worship Mr Roosevelt meant the sermon as well as the liturgy, and if the sermon may be preached, it may be printed and published *urbi et orbi*. Free worship implies free speech. There is a less obvious but no less certain connexion between free worship and the attainment of economic and mental security.[1]

But Mr Addison proceeds too rapidly. No doubt for President Roosevelt in America worship included the sermon, and so freedom of worship includes some freedom of speech and logically should include some freedom of publication. In Eastern Europe, freedom of worship carries no such implications. Worship is the liturgy without the sermon for the Orthodox Church. At least the sermon is of quite subsidiary interest. The positions which Mr Addison would occupy with a rush have to be captured one by one. The absolute minimum of religious liberty is freedom to worship in accord with the convictions and traditions of the group concerned. Some spark of religious liberty exists when

[1] *Religious Equality in Modern England*, pp. 2, 3 (S.P.C.K. 1944).

the group is permitted to meet for worship though only in private, the meetings being confined to known adherents of the group and being open not to the general public but only to police inspection. A fuller measure of liberty is granted when the group is permitted to organize *public* worship. This may still have to be purely liturgical, but if the sermon is recognized as a part of public worship, this will not automatically carry with it the right to further publication. Full religious liberty is much more than freedom of worship. Freedom of speech and freedom of worship are not just conterminous. Freedom of the press, freedom to propagate the faith, freedom to educate in the faith, freedom to express the faith in deeds, in social activities and organization, freedom to organize and control the life of the religious association and to define its faith, economic independence through the ownership of property, and the right to keep in effective touch with fellow-believers in every land—all these elements belong to religious liberty in the full sense of the term. Freedom of worship would have to be very liberally interpreted if it is to include them all. Perhaps logically it does include them all. Nevertheless, they need to be explicitly stated, as is done in the charter of religious freedom issued by the Joint Committee on Religious Liberty.[1]

Religious liberty then admits of many degrees. It may also be subject to certain limitations. In times of crisis, all liberties may have to be restricted. Even Mill

[1] This very important document is printed as an appendix to this book.

allowed this in the case at least of the small city-states of the ancient world.

The ancient commonwealths thought themselves entitled to practise, and the ancient philosophers countenanced, the regulation of every part of private conduct by public authority, on the ground that the State had a deep interest in the whole bodily and mental discipline of every one of its citizens: a mode of thinking which may have been admissible in small republics surrounded by powerful enemies, in constant peril of being subverted by foreign attack or internal commotion, and to which even a short interval of relaxed energy and self-command might so easily be fatal that they could not afford to wait for the salutary permanent effects of freedom.[1]

But apart from times of crisis, some restrictions may legitimately be imposed on the propaganda and conduct of religious bodies. A sentence from the statement on 'Human Rights and Religious Freedom', to which attention has already been drawn, will indicate the kind of restriction which may be justifiable.

We recognize that this right [of religious freedom], while inalienable, is nevertheless in the following sense not an unconditional right: if the adherents of any form of religion so exercise their right of religious freedom as to disturb public order or endanger public security, or outrage the basic moral conceptions which are essential to both, they do so at their own risk, and the State to which they belong, or in which they are resident, is entitled to invoke the sanctions of law against them.[2]

[1] Op. cit. pp. 10, 11.   [2] Statement, p. 4.

Even if the danger of disturbance of public order comes from the public rather than the religious body concerned, the State may still legitimately request the religious body to forgo, at least temporarily, some form of publication or propaganda. Perhaps the reference in the statement to outraging the basic moral conceptions essential to public order and public security is too narrowly conceived. Can any State sanction a return to religious practices now judged to be immoral and inhuman? Whether or not it disturbed public order or endangered public security, no State, we may hope, would permit a revival of human sacrifice. It may be dangerous to admit it and difficult to define it, but the State has some responsibility for resisting moral retrogression in the name of religion, and this may clearly involve some qualifications to the inalienable right of religious liberty.

In so far as religious liberty is a question of rights, it is wrapped up with the constitutional forms of the State and with the policies of governments. But, as Mill argues, we have to consider also the pressures exerted by Society—the problem of maintaining a social atmosphere favourable to religious liberty. In this connexion, the attitude of the adherents of any given religion to the adherents of other religions may be of supreme importance. Similarly the relations of the different groups of those who profess and call themselves Christians to each other will further or hinder the development and maintenance of a genuine toleration. It may even be the case that at the present time a heavier responsibility rests upon the Church than upon the State. We shall have to consider not only what the State should do but also what the Christian Churches should do and what should be expected from the representatives of the living religions of the world.

Chapter II

RELIGIOUS LIBERTY: ITS BASIS AND REASONED DEFENCE

The case for toleration has been and may be argued on many grounds. Of these the respect due to conscience is fundamental. 'The great writers to whom the world owes what religious liberty it possesses, have mostly asserted freedom of conscience as an indefeasible right, and denied absolutely that a human being is accountable to others for his religious belief.'[1] To-day men are sceptical about indefeasible rights and distrust absolute assertions and denials. The claim for religious liberty as well as for other liberties is often denounced as a defence of a discredited individualism. It is merely part of that Anglo-Saxon tradition which, Mr Birdofredum Sawin understood, would break down the morale of the enemy in the war with Mexico. He was told:

That Anglo-Saxondom's idee's a breaking 'em to
    pieces,
An' that idee's that every man doos just wat he
    damn pleases.[2]

An Anglo-Saxon prejudice in favour of irresponsible anarchic individualism—in such terms the plea for religious liberty is described and dismissed.

[1] Mill, *On Liberty*, p. 7.
[2] J. R. Lowell, *Biglow Papers*. In *Poetical Works*, p. 217 (Routledge, 1894).

The standard of the Rights of Man was raised by men who regarded the individual as prior to the State, and who were in revolt against governments which they regarded as tyrannical. This temper is discernible alike in the American Declaration of Independence and in the French Declaration of the Rights of Man.

We hold these truths to be self-evident: that all men are created equal: that they are endowed by their Creator with inalienable rights: that among these rights are life, liberty and the pursuit of happiness: that, to secure these rights, governments are instituted among men, deriving their just powers from the consent of the governed: that, whenever any form of government becomes destructive of these ends, it is the right of the people to alter or abolish it and to institute new government, laying its foundations on such principles and organizing all its powers in such form as to them shall seem most likely to effect their safety and happiness.

The philosophy which inspires the French Declaration speaks more readily of Nature than of the Creator. Rousseau's 'Man is born free but everywhere he is in chains' is an assertion of natural rights. It is an appeal to a Law of Nature or rather to an idealized primitive state of Nature. 'In all the speculations of Rousseau, the central figure whether arrayed in an English dress as the signatory of a social compact, or simply stripped naked of all historical qualities, is uniformly Man, in a supposed state of nature.'[1]

The thought-forms adopted in these Declarations and the assumptions underlying them are no longer

---

[1] Maine, *Ancient Law*, p. 88 (ed. 1894).

fashionable or defensible. Man is not born free. He would not be born at all, save as a member of a family subject to parental authority. Neither the doctrine of natural rights nor the theory of the origin of the State in a social contract is tenable to-day. Freedom is not so natural and the State with its authority is not so artificial as these doctrines assume. Yet these doctrines were not invented primarily in the interests of private enterprise in business or to foster anarchic individualism. They were promulgated to defend the common man against tyranny. If the defence be inadequate the cause is not thereby discredited. The force of the Declarations rests on the conviction that governments are made for men, not men for governments. As Thomas Aquinas puts it, *Civis regitur in commodum suum, non in commodum magistratus.* ('The citizen is governed in his own interest, not in the interest of the ruler.')

To appeal to Nature as a guarantee of either freedom or equality is a hazardous proceeding. Since Darwin, we have been inclined to identify the Law of Nature with the Law of the Jungle, and the classic form of Darwinism, with its emphasis on the struggle for existence and the survival of the fittest, seems to underwrite the power-politics of Machiavelli. The doctrine that might is right leaves the majority of men little hope of freedom or of equality save as slaves. Attempts to interpret the nature of Society or the State in accordance with concepts of Nature drawn from particular sciences are equally disappointing. The social contract theory of the State seemed akin to earlier theories of the atomic structure of the universe. The State was the result of a fortuitous concourse of human atoms. A form of democracy may be built on such atomic individualism, but it does justice neither to the individual nor to the State. To borrow analogies from the biologist and regard the State as an organism inevitably leads to subordinating the individual to the State. The individual has no significance save in the light of his function as a citizen, whatever that may happen to be. The rights of the individual will be little respected where such a conception of the State prevails. Nevertheless, Dr Julian Huxley, in his Romanes Lecture, thinks the study of evolution may provide some support for freedom and for equality of opportunity. The thin line of progress culminates in man and henceforward progress must be social rather than strictly biological. But the line of progress in evolution suggests that, negatively, warfare within a species is normally a great obstacle to progress and that, positively, the encouragement of variation in the individual members of the species is an essential condition of progress. For Dr Julian Huxley this means that religious liberty must be safeguarded, since he considers religious experience, particularly mystical experience, to possess intrinsic value. If then we may assume that progress is desirable and that humanity as a whole is to share in it, the study of evolution may be held to provide some support for the cause of liberty in general and of religious liberty in particular.

This appeal to Nature will not bear the weight

Dr Julian Huxley attaches to it. Social progress is no doubt biologically conditioned: it is not biologically determined. The ideals Dr Julian Huxley entertains for Society are not derived from his biology. It is best to state these ideals clearly apart from any doctrine of creation such as was invoked by the framers of the Declaration of Independence and apart from any speculations as to the position of Man in a state of Nature. As Susan Stebbing made clear in her book, *Ideals and Illusions*, the moral principle asserted in the Declaration is simply this, 'all men alike ought to be free and happy'.[1] Later she expands it in these terms: 'All men, whatsoever may be their race, skin-colour, social status, creed, mental or physical ability, ought to lead free and happy lives, ought—that is—to be free each to shape his own mode of living in accordance with his own abilities and needs.'[2] This principle if accepted carries with it the case for religious liberty. A man must be free to shape his mode of living in accordance with his creed. Societies will be judged by their success or failure in assuring this freedom. Miss Stebbing indicated a still stronger moral basis for religious liberty when she wrote:

It is no illusion but uncontested fact that here and now we know that hatred, cruelty, intolerance and indifference to human misery are evil: that love, kindliness, tolerance, forgiveness and truth are good, so unquestionably good that we do not need God or heaven to assure us of their worth.[3]

[1] Op. cit. p. 53.   [2] Op. cit. p. 55.
[3] Op. cit. p. 200.

I believe Miss Stebbing was justified in saying 'we know' in this connexion. Such judgements may be intuitive but they are still judgements, and true judgements at that. Yet in some quarters, the possibility of ethical knowledge or of objectively valid ethical judgements is vigorously denied, and quite clearly there are situations in which men forget if they do not deny these particular ethical judgements. The devotees of power-politics, whether they be violent social revolutionaries or aggressive nationalists, make virtues of hatred, cruelty, intolerance and indifference to human misery, and discount love, kindliness, tolerance, forgiveness and truth as weak sentimentalism. Even defenders of freedom and independence against aggression, while still agreeing in principle with Miss Stebbing, falter in their rejection of evil and in their loyalty to good. Nevertheless those who share these intuitive judgements are morally bound by them. And as Mr Lionel Elwin contends, educationists might agree in commending such standards, even if philosophers cannot reach agreement as to the metaphysical or theological implications of such standards. At the same time we cannot but seek support in reason and experience for our moral intuitions. The appeal to history may be more successful than the appeal to Nature.

It is sometimes supposed that the lessons of history are all negative. The historian can confidently label blind alleys. He cannot as confidently point out the right road. The story of the past contains many warnings if we would but heed them. History does not show that persecution and intolerance can never succeed. It does show that success in suppressing religious liberty is more prejudicial to the welfare of a people than failure could have been.' But Mr A. L. Rowse would not confine the historian to negative warnings. 'We may as historians condemn Nero for a bad man and acclaim Jesus Christ as a good man.' 'Historical thinking can tell you...that the Christian doctrine of love among men is a better basis for human relations in a society than envy and hatred.'[1] History does provide some evidence for the view put forward by Mr Addison that freedom of worship is essential to the achievement and maintenance of all other freedoms. Nevertheless, the survey of the past experience of mankind is neither the source of our moral standards nor their final justification, though the spectacle of rough justice which it constantly presents may be a warning to moral reactionaries and a cordial to the drooping spirits of those who believe that only righteousness exalteth a nation.

Further support for religious liberty and for the moral convictions set forth in Miss Stebbing's book may be derived from the consideration of the nature of science in general. As on critical reflexion it is clear that any form of Naturalism arising from a particular science, e.g. physics or biology, will be found to be incompatible with the nature of science in general, since scientific inquiry is a spiritual activity of persons, so also it is clear that the strict impartiality enjoined on scientists in particular fields of inquiry does not mean

[1] *The Use of History*, pp. 152, 153.

that science is morally neutral or indifferent, this very impartiality being the moral obligation to be intellectually honest. The existence and the progress of natural science are morally conditioned. All scientific inquiry involves and requires a moral discipline. The faith and morality implicit in natural science have recently been expounded by Professor Michael Polanyi in his Riddell Lectures on *Science, Faith and Society*. The main thesis of the book is that the realm of science depends on a particular form of faith, that this faith creates a society which in turn guards, hands on and develops the faith. This faith he defines in a fourfold proposition: (1) that there is such a thing as truth; (2) that all members of the confraternity of science love it; (3) that they feel obliged to pursue it; and (4) are in fact capable of pursuing it. There is a general authority in the realm of science, an authority which all recognize and in which all share. It is not a specific authority concentrated in a single head or council. Its maintenance and right exercise depend on strict conscientiousness, on the love of truth and on the sense of obligation to pursue it. Fairness and tolerance are of the essence of the scientific spirit. Fairness means distinguishing one's evidence from one's judgement and one's judgement from one's personal feelings and interests in presenting one's case. Tolerance means examining patiently and sympathetically the case presented by another, whatever its confusion and defects may be, so as not to overlook the truth it may contain. The authority attaching to the findings of science is only respected because such findings are always open to re-examination and revision. Freedom of inquiry is the vital breath of seekers after truth.

In thus making explicit the acceptance of strict moral obligation which is implicit in the nature of science in general, Professor Polanyi is helping to heal the division between science and religion which is the real crisis in Western culture. The value of such a contribution is manifest when we find so brilliant a thinker as Mr Bertrand Russell assuming that to deny objective validity to all ethical judgements and to treat them as purely emotional is compatible with his loyalty to science—a loyalty depending on an ethical judgement whose objective validity he cannot reasonably deny. Perhaps Mr Russell was also too precipitate in assuming that in a society organized by science the welfare and worth of the individual would count for little. There is such a danger, in so far as science isolates love of truth from love, kindliness and forgiveness in our dealings with our fellowmen. But tolerance at least is essential to science, and a genuinely scientific society must insist on the fullest measure of religious liberty. It may confidently be affirmed that so long as men retain the true scientific spirit they will maintain freedom of religion. It may also be confidently affirmed that if men become indifferent to freedom of religion, they will not retain unimpaired the true scientific spirit.

For the Christian, the basis of religious liberty is to be found first in the purpose of God in creating man, that is, in man's nature and in his unique status in creation, and second in the sacred mystery of redemption, whereby God in Christ is reconciling the world to Himself.

In Christian belief the essential meaning of all human freedom is freedom to live according to the will of God, which includes the opportunity to exercise and develop in full measure the capacities with which He has endowed human nature, and a corresponding deliverance from conditions which thwart His purpose for mankind.[1]

To man are given the privilege and the responsibility of exercising a certain measure of lordship in the realm of Nature and of enjoying a measure of creative activity. Freedom and spontaneity are vital for the realization of God's purpose for mankind. The Christian will find allies in all who recognize the unique status of man and the essentially spiritual nature of man, even though they do not share the Christian faith in a personal God, the maker of heaven and earth. Thus, Croce, writing of the religion of liberty, rediscovers and reaffims the saying of Vico 'that the republic sought by Plato was nothing but the course of human events'. In the light of this saying

man no longer looked on himself as belittled by history or as vindicating himself against it and pushing the past away from him as a shameful memory. Instead, a true and tireless creator, he looked on himself in the history of the world as he looked on himself in his own life. No longer did history appear destitute of spirituality and abandoned to blind forces or sustained and constantly directed by alien forces. Now it was

---

[1] *Human Rights and Religious Freedom*, p. 3.

seen to be the work and the activity of the spirit, and so, *since spirit is liberty, the work of liberty*.[1]

In this conception, Croce is exposing the fallacy involved in historical materialism. The materialist conception of history rightly emphasizes the economic basis of society and the far-reaching importance of changes in the technique of production. But it misunderstands the character of men's economic activities. The economic life of humanity is not pervaded throughout by necessity. Invention is the work and activity of the spirit and, since spirit is liberty, the work of liberty. Genius and originality can never flourish under tyranny. To realize that history is the realm of man's creative activity, the scene of the successes and failures of rational morally responsible agents, should commit one to the cause of religious liberty. To embrace the materialist conception of history, to regard men as the willing or unwilling agents in a predetermined process based on the working of the laws of physical necessity is naturally associated with the denial of all kinds of freedom. The Christian at any rate will start from the doctrine of creation. He will agree with Milton that 'no man who knows aught, can be so stupid as to deny that all men naturally were born free, being the image and resemblance of God himself'.[2] If as John Morley says, Milton here anticipates Rousseau, Rousseau watered down Milton by omitting the reference to man as

---

[1] *History of Europe*, pp. 8, 9.
[2] T. R. Glover, *Poets and Puritans*, p. 57.

the image and resemblance of God himself. Even the American Declaration of Independence, with its phrase 'endowed by their Creator' does not rise to the height of Milton's argument or the level of his conviction.

As Locke cogently argued, the case for religious liberty follows from the need of sincerity in religion if it is to be genuine, and from the nature of the Christian religion in particular.

No man can, if he would, conform his religion to the dictates of another. All the life and power of truth consist in the inward and full persuasion of the mind: and faith is not faith without believing. Whatever profession we make, to whatever outward worship we conform, if we are not fully satisfied in our own mind that the one is true and the other well pleasing unto God, such profession and such practice far from being any furtherance, are indeed great obstacles to our salvation.[1]

The denial of religious liberty fosters hypocrisy and unreality. The saying attributed to Bishop Thirlwall is still worth remembering. When a don argued for compulsory attendance at College chapel on the ground that we have to choose between compulsory religion or no religion at all, Thirlwall observed that he could not see the distinction.

Again Locke argues forcibly that intolerance and persecution, with all their attendant cruelties, are inconsistent with the charity which is the essential mark

[1] *Civil Government*, by John Locke, p. 127 (Blackwell, 1946).

of a Christian. Some of William Penn's aphorisms state the case effectively.

Grace perfects, but never sours or spoils nature.

To be unnatural in defence of grace, is a contradiction.

Hardly anything looks worse than to defend religion by ways that show it has no credit with us.

To be *furious* in religion is to be irreligiously religious.

If he that is without bowels is not a man, how, then, can he be a Christian?

It were better to be of *no* church, than to be bitter for *any*.

Some folk think they may scold, rail, hate, rob and kill too: so it be for God's sake. But nothing in us, unlike him, can please him.

For the Christian, the final argument for religious freedom comes from the manner of our redemption. The gospel of the grace of God is indeed so amazing that most Christians are but half-convinced. Anything like adequate expression of what St Paul calls the ministry of reconciliation is rare in Christian literature. There is a great passage in the letter to Diognetus, where the writer grasps the significance of this aspect of the Incarnation. After insisting that in Jesus, God sent his Creative Word to dwell with us, the writer continues:

Well then, did God send him as any man might expect to play the dictator and inspire fear and terror? By no means, but in sweet-reasonableness and gentleness he sent him, as a king sending a royal son, as God

he sent him, as a man to men he sent him, as saving
he sent him, as persuading, not violently compelling:
for violence belongeth not to God. He sent him
to call men, not to drive them, in love and not in
judgement.[1]

Such a characterization of the Incarnation determines
the nature of the ministry of reconciliation entrusted
to the Church.

Origen's comment on the glory of omnipotence is
in line with this, though he is stressing wisdom rather
than love.

God the Father is almighty because he holds
dominion over all things, that is, over heaven and
earth, sun, moon and stars and everything contained
in them. This dominion he exercises through his Word,
for 'in the name of Jesus every knee bows, of things
in heaven and things on earth and things under the
earth'. Now if every knee bows to Jesus, then un-
doubtedly it is Jesus to whom all things have been
subjected, and it is he who wields dominion over all
things and all things have been subjected to the Father
through him: for it is through wisdom, that is *by word
and reason and not by force and necessity* that they are
subject. His glory, therefore, lies in the very fact that
he possesses all things: and this is the purest and
brightest glory of omnipotence, that the universe is
held in subjection by reason and wisdom and not by
force and necessity. It is called the 'purest and
brightest' glory of wisdom as the most suitable for
distinguishing it from that glory which is not pure or
sincere.[2]

---

[1] *Ep. ad Diog. c.* 7.
[2] Origen, *On First Principles* (trans. by Butterworth), p. 25
(S.P.C.K. 1936).

If the creation is subject to wisdom rather than to force and necessity, force and necessity are even more clearly alien to the loving wisdom of our God in man's redemption. A closer parallel to the letter to Diognetus may be found in the last recorded utterance of James Nayler, the Quaker evangelist who suffered such a cruel punishment in the time of the Commonwealth for an exhibition of religious enthusiasm which was naturally regarded as blasphemous in Puritan circles. The spirit in which he bore his punishment and the truth he learned from it are reflected in this paragraph:

There is a spirit which I feel, that delights to do no evil nor to revenge any wrong, but delights to endure all things in hope to enjoy its own in the end. Its hope is to outlive all wrath and contention and to weary out all exaltation and cruelty or whatever is of a nature contrary to itself. It sees to the end of all temptations: As it bears no evil in itself, so it conceives none in thoughts to any other: If it be betrayed, it bears it: for its ground and spring is the mercies and forgiveness of God. Its crown is meekness, its life is everlasting love unfeigned, and it takes its kingdom with entreaty and not with contention, and keeps it by lowliness of mind.[1]

It is thus that Christ takes and keeps his kingdom in the hearts and minds of men.

There is a paradox in the ministry of reconciliation. 'God in Christ was reconciling the world to himself....We are Christ's ambassadors, then, and

---

[1] See *The Spirit of Man*, ed. by Robert Bridges, extract No. 372—the only extract from a Quaker source in this famous anthology.

God appeals to you through us: we entreat you in Christ's name, make your peace with God.' God appeals, in Christ's name we entreat—that is the paradox. Any man would expect that God would command, God would compel. But no, God is the suppliant. Since God in Christ persuades, men may not, in Christ's name, compel. To deny religious liberty is to deny Christ.

Chapter III

RELIGIOUS LIBERTY IN THE
MODERN WORLD

Religious liberty is imperilled by many important developments in the political world of to-day. The advances in the direction of toleration in the eighteenth and nineteenth centuries were due not so much to religious indifference as to the assumption that the distinctive spheres of Church and State could be clearly defined. The principle, 'A Free Church in a Free State', seemed to Liberals to be an adequate guide. The confidence with which John Locke asserted the claims of religious liberty depended on his clear definition of the purposes of civil government. 'The commonwealth seems to me to be a society of men constituted *only* for the procuring, preserving and advancing their own civil interests. Civil interests I call life, liberty, health and indolency of body: and the possession of outward things, such as money, lands, houses, furniture and the like.'[1] If civil government could keep its activities within the limits of Locke's 'only', religious liberty would not be in jeopardy. Christ's saying, 'Render unto Caesar the things that are Caesar's and unto God the things that are God's', leaves the things that are Caesar's undefined. If, as Lord Acton remarks, this saying gave the State a sanctity it had not previously enjoyed and

[1] Op. cit. p. 126.

limits it had not previously recognized, the nature of
the limits had still to be explored. Locke's conception
of such limits underlay the theory and practice of
laisser-faire radicalism. The function of the State is to
provide defence against external foes and to administer justice. Anything beyond this is *ultra vires*.
But even Locke's definition would justify and require
positive action of the Commonwealth in the interests
of health and material well-being. He leaves at least
a loophole for the entrance of the social-service State,
and the social conditions created by the Industrial
Revolution forced on the development of such a State.
The functions of the State were never at any time
strictly confined to the maintenance of order, the
administration of justice and the defence of the realm.
The suppression of the monasteries and the first
enclosure movement in Tudor times compelled the
civil authority to tackle the problem of poor relief.
The beginnings of the social-service State may be
found in the Poor Law. But the Industrial Revolution
led the State to undertake larger responsibilities and
more far-reaching interventions. The liberty of action
and movement, which Adam Smith claimed for both
master and man, had been advocated primarily in the
interests of the small-scale producer. It tended to be
monopolized by big business. The settlement of wages
and conditions of labour by supposedly free negotia-
tion between individual employers and individual
workers turned out to be anything but equitable in
practice, owing to the disparity in bargaining power of
the parties to the contract. The disparity was only

tardily and partially redressed when Trade Unions asserted and secured the right of collective bargaining. It is unnecessary to recall the history of factory legislation in this country. The State intervened to protect first of all women and children from ruthless exploitation and then to limit the hours of labour for all and to establish minimum conditions for the maintenance of health. This and similar developments were accompanied, and indeed often inspired, by the Idealist theory of the State, which repudiated the atomic individualism of the Radicals and of the theorists of the Social Contract, and which emphasized in its stead the dependence of the individual on Society and the reciprocal responsibilities of both individual and Society. Interest in Greek ideals of citizenship revived. The State exists not only to ensure men's physical existence but also to enable them to live well in the cultural sense. It is important to recognize that the Idealist theory of the State commended and helped to create the social-service State. If it demanded from the individual citizen a respect for and loyalty to the State little short of Burke's impassioned conservatism, it did so because it believed in the immense possibilities of the State as the instrument of brotherhood, as the nurse of the citizen's truest welfare and highest interests. Hegel himself saw that the growing inequality of wealth between the rich and the poor in the U.S.A. would compel the State to intervene, not necessarily, as Mr Laski with his Marxist obsession assumes, to protect the rich against revolutionary violence from the side of the poor, but to protect the poor against

economic exploitation by the rich.[1] He was probably
anticipating anti-trust legislation and the New Deal.
To represent the Idealist theory as intended to maintain
the domination of the property-owning classes is
a misunderstanding. The Idealist theory was not
devised as a bulwark against social revolution. It
provided a philosophic defence of social progress
through the agency of the State which progress, if
achieved, would make violent revolution indefensible
and inexcusable. It favoured and did not retard the
advance of genuinely democratic Socialism. If it underrated the elements of truth in the Marxist theory of the
State as the instrument of class domination, it at least
avoided the errors in which the Marxist theory is
involved.

If the State is not to be confined to merely negative
functions, securing to the individual inalienable rights
and liberties, if it is to undertake more positive duties
to promote the good life, it will inevitably enter the
field of education. As inevitably the State's entry into
this field provokes tension if not conflict in the relations
of Church and State. The Churches may be willing and
even glad to surrender to the State some of the charitable activities which they previously discharged, but
they can never entrust their interest in education
unreservedly and unconditionally to the State. Every
advance on the part of the State in Great Britain from
the first modest grant of £30,000 to be administered
in aid of the voluntary organizations, has been jealously
watched by Church leaders. F. D. Maurice insisted

[1] Laski, *The State in Theory and Practice*, p. 328.

that education must be the work of the Church. 'The Church must educate. A people cannot be educated aright by its political rulers or government.' What he was really contending for was the integrity and independence of the scholar and the teacher. Just as the administration of law and justice must not be subordinated to the immediate interests of political rulers or perverted by *raisons d'État*, so the members of the teaching profession must not be the obsequious servants of State or agents of party propaganda. The Churches have sometimes threatened the intellectual integrity of the teacher, but in refusing to surrender education to the State, they are defending the teacher against a more serious threat to his liberty.

This inevitable tension between Church and State in the field of education is not yet resolved. Attempts to resolve it have taken the form of proposals to divide the territory. Let the State confine its activities to elementary education—the inculcation of the notorious three R's. Or let the State concentrate on safe, non-controversial studies, like mathematics, physics and chemistry. Again, the State might be asked to deal with matters of fact, with the collection and dissemination of factual information. In the State-system of education the scholar should become acquainted with data, not with judgements or beliefs. Finally, many have nursed the hope of distinguishing and then separating secular from religious education. Let the State provide secular education for all and let the Church provide religious education for those who desire it.

All these suggestions break down, because education, if it is to be genuine and worth while, is one and indivisible. True education means character-training. G. Bernard Shaw, in the preface to *On the Rocks*, argues forcibly that for education a standard religion is indispensable.

All will agree to exterminate illiteracy by compulsory reading, writing and arithmetic: indeed they have already done so. But all will not agree on a standard religion. Yet a standard religion is indispensable, however completely it may shed the old theologies. *Every attempt to banish religion from the schools proves that in this respect Nature abhors a vacuum*, and that the community must make up its mind, or have its mind made up for it by its official thinkers, as to what its children are to be taught to believe and how they should be trained to behave.

Mr Shaw goes on to argue that

Compromise is ruled out by the nature of the case.... What compromise is possible between myself, for instance, who believe in the religion of Creative Evolution, the economics of Socialism and a diet from which the dead bodies of men, fish, fowls and animals are rigidly excluded, and my Fundamentalist neighbours who believe that all Evolutionists go to hell: that children languish and die without beef-steaks: and that without private property civilization must perish? We cannot exterminate one another at present: but the time cannot be very far off when the education authorities will have to consider which set of beliefs is the better qualification for citizenship in Utopia.[1]

[1] *Too True to be Good, etc.* p. 167.

Fortunately education authorities are not obliged to choose between such dismal alternatives as Fundamentalism and Shavianism. But State education will involve the adoption and inculcation of some moral standards, and though this may not at once be obvious, such standards will require some philosophic justification. If the standards in question are approximately Christian, the Christian faith will be found to be indispensable for their maintenance. In the mid-Victorian period, the separation of Church and State seemed to Dissenters and Radicals to be the grand, indeed the paramount question of the hour.[1] To-day the grand question is, in what ways and on what conditions should Church and State co-operate in the field of education? While there will necessarily be some limits to toleration and to equality of treatment, it is not true that 'compromise is ruled out by the nature of the case'. On the contrary, compromise is in practice inevitable, and any compromise may involve some limitation of the full liberty which a religious body claims or desires for itself. Every such limitation must be carefully scrutinized. Thus, the State may legitimately prefer to entrust education to laymen, but ought the exclusion of religious orders from participation in education as in France or the exclusion of men in orders from the State secondary schools as in this country, to be accepted without question? But where the State is not committed to an anti-religious or anti-Christian position, where a people is still attached to the idea of a Christian society, the

[1] Cf. Addison, *Religious Equality in Modern England*, p. 86.

extent of co-operation between Church and State depends more on the Church than the State. The Churches must put their house in order. The greater the measure of agreement among the Churches, the easier it is for the State to invite and utilize the co-operation of the Churches.

There are difficulties and dangers for religious liberty in the development of the social-service State, but naturally the most serious menace lies in the emergence of totalitarian régimes committed to anti-religious or anti-Christian philosophies. Such régimes whether Fascist or Communist seek to exclude the Church from the field of education. It is a vital necessity for a totalitarian State to secure its hold on youth. If the Church is not absolutely forbidden to promote social and educational activities among young people, organizations like the Hitler Youth or the Komsomol are so run as to ensure that the Church has no opportunity of effective contact. There are other ways of stifling the influence of the Church than active, violent persecution. Hitler confidently expected to undermine the Christian Church, both Catholic and Reformed, in Germany. Lenin was equally resolved on rooting out religion from the life of the Russian people. If the frontal attack of anti-God propaganda has proved a failure and if the position of the Orthodox Church has become easier during the war and since, the Communists are still bent on making Marxist-Leninism the faith of the State. Dialectical Materialism is the standard religion which the official thinkers of the Party have imposed on the Russian people, and all the resources of the national system of education are devoted to securing its acceptance. Wherever a totalitarian régime is established, religious liberties are always limited and such liberties as are granted are only held on sufferance. Moreover, in the present stage of world history, totalitarian régimes are strongly tempted to become imperialist. Economically, the world is becoming increasingly one. Political unity is felt to be more and more necessary. On all sides men talk of world-government. Naturally those who believe they have the true basis for a world-order are tempted to impose it by force. Any totalitarian régime may essay to solve the problem of establishing a world-civilization, but the Communist-State is in any case committed to a programme of world-revolution. The advocates of such a programme cannot be squeamish in dealing with religious faiths. For them 'he that is not with us is against us' is clearly the directive. Religious toleration can at best be only a matter of expediency under such a régime.

It is, however, highly improbable that any totalitarian régime will succeed in dominating mankind. It is so improbable that the strongest of them may not even attempt it. The great obstacle to any such enterprise is the strength of national feeling. The age of national States is not over, and in India and Pakistan we have fresh accessions to the number of such States. Both these States exhibit the close association of national consciousness with a particular religious faith which creates obvious dangers for religious liberty. In Moslem countries in particular the strength of national feeling reinforces religious intolerance. The assertion of human rights will be no easy matter in the modern world. Freedom of religion will not readily be conceded. Indeed, of the four freedoms it may be the most difficult to establish.

CHAPTER IV

RELIGIOUS LIBERTY BEHIND
THE IRON CURTAIN

THE main sources of religious intolerance are four in number. There is, first, religious bigotry. Next comes the reaction of secularist rationalism, expressed in the extremes of anti-clericalism. National feeling, in the third place, may find a weapon for defence or aggression in associating itself with a particular faith. In the fourth place, social revolutionaries regard traditional religious faiths and institutions as obstacles which may have to be swept violently on one side. All these elements combine to determine the attitude of the Communist Party in Russia towards the Churches and towards the Christian faith. The familiar description of religion as the opiate of the people embodies the outlook of the revolutionary. According to Lenin 'the roots of religion are in the social degradation of the toiling masses and their seeming impotence before the blind forces of capitalism'. 'All contemporary religions and churches, all and every kind of religious organization, Marxism has always viewed as organs of bourgeois reaction, serving as a defence of exploitation and the doping of the working-class.' While, as we shall see, this analysis does not necessarily commit the Marxist to ruthless persecution, which may not be expedient, it does mean that Lenin would tolerate no tenderness towards religion within the

3-2

Communist Party. When Lunacharsky and Maxim Gorki appealed to the Marxist formula that religion is to be regarded as a private matter (*privat-sache*) as permitting a positive attitude to religion on the part of the individual Marxist, Lenin indignantly denied this. Christian admirers of the Russian experiment often ask whether one cannot be both Christian and Communist. Lenin's answer is clear: it is impossible. As social revolutionaries, the Communists cannot tolerate Christianity. They are the less inclined to do so because Marxism inherits the secular-rationalist tradition. Marx and Engels were, in respect of one side of their characters, typical bourgeois rationalists, as blind as any other bourgeois free-thinkers to the true nature of religion. As Jacques Maritain observes, it is a pity the working-class movement should be burdened with one of the stupidest elements in nineteenth-century culture, bourgeois free-thought, but this is part of the Marxist tradition. Where the commonplaces of Victorian rationalist propaganda are treated as axioms, the atmosphere can hardly be favourable to religious liberty. This combination of social revolutionary enthusiasm with secularist rationalism is also seeking a marriage with national feeling. Perhaps every nation from time to time indulges in Messianism, and each nation may be justified in believing or at least hoping that it will have some distinctive contribution to make to human welfare. Milton magnificently assumes that when God intends a new beginning of any kind, he speaks first to his Englishmen. There is in Russia a belief that the people have a Messianic destiny, and many believe that the Communist revolution constitutes the Russian contribution to human welfare. The faith that inspires and guides the revolution has then a claim to an exclusive loyalty. To propagate it and discourage all other creeds is an obvious duty. And finally Communism has become a religion, so that a religious fanaticism is added to the other three factors which influence the policy of the Government of the U.S.S.R.

Whether the Iron Curtain is really an iron curtain, or whether it be made of some lighter and more easily penetrable material, there can be no question as to the nature of the cultural revolution which is proceeding behind it. What is being attempted throughout Eastern Europe is well characterized in a striking paragraph from Mr Kingsley Martin's 'Curtain Diary' in the *New Statesman and Nation* of 12 June 1948:

My friend Leo Murray, who, like most other *Manchester Guardian* correspondents, is more interested in learning and understanding the facts than in propaganda, has made the good point that what we are really witnessing throughout Eastern Europe is the more or less 'forcible conversion' of the population. This is the root of the matter. The real object is to bring up a new generation to believe in a new religion. The methods used are very similar to those of the counter-Reformation which won back Protestant countries to loyalty to the Vatican. Jobs for the faithful: the deprivation of the normal means of livelihood for the recalcitrant: force and the Inquisition when nothing else will serve. Marxism is now a very complete religion: it has its sacred books, its dogmas and philosophy, its libraries of disputation, its martyrs and its heretics. The gospel is spread by a single party whose methods and discipline remind one forcibly of the Jesuit Order. Its object is to substitute science and Marxian order for revelation and clerical control. Such a wide ambition can only be fulfilled by extreme simplification of doctrine. The masses must be convinced by propaganda. The back-sliders must be punished: the faithful must be disciplined. For the masses the propaganda must be as black and white as that favoured by Reaction itself. . . . The simplicity and dogmatism of propaganda is to me the least palatable aspect of this process of conversion.

In view of this attempt at forcible conversion, the outlook for religious liberty may seem wellnigh hopeless. Actually the situation is not as hopeless as it seems at first sight. In Russia itself after a period in which there was actual persecution, and in which strong support was given to anti-God propaganda, the liberty of worship granted in the constitution has been generally respected and to-day the attitude of the government is more friendly to the Churches, at least to the Orthodox Church, than ever before. There are many reasons for this. The hold of religion on the masses of the people was found to be stronger than the authorities expected. The anti-God propaganda failed in its object. People were neither to be laughed nor argued out of their religion. Then the part played by the Orthodox Church in sustaining morale during the war secured for it a deeper respect and further liberties. The way was open for a new assessment of the contribution of the Church to Russian life and character, in the past as well as in the present. But apart from this,

Lenin saw the unwisdom of direct attacks on popular beliefs and practices. His analysis of the roots of religion pointed to another technique than violent repression. If the roots of religion are in the social degradation of the toiling masses, you have only to end that social degradation, and religion like the State will wither away. The expectation may be as groundless in the one case as in the other, but so long as Communists entertain this expectation, they will not feel bound to persecute the Christian Church. So at present the policy of the Communists towards the Orthodox Churches at least is one of appeasement. Their attitude towards the Roman Catholic Church is not so cordial, but they do not despair of finding a *modus vivendi* with local Catholic groups, though they may neither desire nor seek a concordat with the Vatican.

The more benevolent attitude of the Russian government towards the Orthodox Church and the effects of it, as they have developed during the war and since, are well described by Mr John Fischer in *The Scared Men in the Kremlin*, where he gives the impressions he formed while on an U.N.R.R.A. mission to the Ukraine in the spring of 1946:

The nearest thing to real independence and virility in the Ukrainian culture probably is the Orthodox Church. It not only has survived two decades of suppression and anti-religious propaganda: it even seemed to thrive under persecution, as Christian churches have done before.

In the end the Politburo finally remembered that venerable political maxim, 'If you can't lick 'em, join 'em'; and shortly before the beginning of the war it made a deal with the priesthood. The Church promised to give its wholehearted support to the Soviet régime; and in return the government shut off its anti-religious propaganda, disbanded the League of Militant Atheists, reopened some eight thousand churches, authorized the training of priests in theological seminaries, and permitted believers to worship unmolested.

A notable advance in education for the ministry was reported by Dr Hromadka, Dean of the Hus Faculty in Prague, when he returned from a visit to the U.S.S.R. at the beginning of this year (1948). 'The number of seminaries (for the training of priests) is growing and two higher theological academies have been opened for the training of seminary Professors and higher clergy.' I understand that Berdyaev was invited to return to teach in one of these academies, but he declined, either because of increasing years or because he still distrusted the Communist régime.

The reopening of churches, according to John Fischer, evoked a response which surprised even the clergy. 'People flocked back into the arms of the Church literally by the millions.' At the cathedral in Kiev

Sunday services had to be run off in relays from daybreak to dusk in order to accommodate all of the worshippers. On Easter morning the Cathedral was packed to the doors before dawn and some four thousand people stood on the grounds outside.... These were not merely old folks or unenlightened peasants; they were of all ages and classes, many of them well dressed and obviously prosperous. Among them were a number of Red Army officers, ranging up to the rank of full colonel.

This kind of scene is not confined to Kiev or the Ukraine, or to the year 1946. The return to the Church is evident in other parts of Russia and still continues. If attendance at public worship be the measure of Christianity, Russia is probably the most Christian country in Europe to-day. The opportunity for advance is not confined to the Orthodox Church. The Praesidium of the United Council of the Baptist and Evangelical Christians of the U.S.S.R. issued a statement in the second half of 1946 which affirms that the Protestant group in the U.S.S.R. has

complete religious freedom to carry out its activity day after day. Because of this freedom we have a flourishing spiritual life in our churches. There is a great fire that burns in the hearts of our believers. The Gospel is preached freely and thousands of sinners repent and turn to Christ. There is not a single church of ours which does not have its conversions. We have information that during the first half of the summer of 1946 already thirty thousand newly converted souls were baptized.

Since under the pre-war constitution the only religious liberty conceded was liberty of worship, the Churches being denied the right of propaganda and publication and being forbidden to organize social and educational activities, it is interesting to note that the Baptists are now permitted to publish a journal, and are also publishing Bibles, New Testaments and books of spiritual songs. These books of course may be regarded as service-books, books required for public worship, whose use was permitted under the pre-war constitution. But the Baptists now seem able to publish and distribute these more freely than before. They are also engaging in charitable work. 'Regular monthly offerings are made in all our churches for the children of soldiers who died during the war. These offerings provide large funds.'[1] So far as I know, there is still no evidence that the embargo on Sunday schools and youth clubs run by the Churches has been lifted, and it is noteworthy that the Russian Baptists were not allowed to send representatives to the International Baptists' Congress at Copenhagen in July 1947.[2] It remains to be seen how many of the Churches behind the Iron Curtain will be represented at Amsterdam. Many of its leaders would wish the Russian Church to participate in the World Council of Churches, but this may not commend itself to the government of the U.S.S.R. Contact with the West does not at the

[1] *Christianity and Crisis*, 23 June 1947.

[2] At the Baptist Church House the general impression of the position of Baptists in Russia is not so favourable as the particulars in the text would suggest. The authorities there say: 'We have no information as to the amount of religious liberty allowed in Soviet Russia, beyond the fact that public worship is permitted. Sunday schools are not allowed, nor any meetings for young people or women. The Russian Baptists are allowed to issue a bi-monthly magazine entitled *Bratsky Vestnik* but it is censored and largely reflects the Government outlook. The membership of Baptist churches was reckoned before the war as over 1,000,000 but now they claim only 300,000. We have no knowledge of what has happened to the others. None of the preachers taken from their churches to exile or imprisonment, has been allowed to return.'

moment suit Russian policy. But since the States of Eastern Europe form a Slav block, 'the Church is now serving as a useful instrument of Soviet foreign policy among Orthodox Slavs'. Russian delegates may not attend at Amsterdam, but representatives of Orthodox Churches outside Russia are welcome to confer in Moscow.

Such a conference was held in July this year, when the Russian Orthodox Church celebrated the 500th anniversary of its existence as an independent Church. For the Orthodox Churches this meeting provided the same opportunity for consultation and decisions as Lambeth offered at the same time to the Anglican Communion. The decision as to attendance at Amsterdam was taken then.[1] The Patriarch Alexius told a Reuter correspondent in May 1948, that the Russian Church had the benevolent support of Stalin and the Soviet Government and enjoyed complete freedom in organizing its internal affairs. But contact with Churches in the West is not an internal affair, and the benevolence of the Soviet Government will not necessarily sanction participation in the work of the World Council of Churches.

Reviewing the information that has come to hand

[1] At the time of writing, it was expected that representatives would attend Amsterdam from Czechoslovakia, Hungary, Roumania and Yugoslavia. The Jewish World Congress, held at Montreux in July 1948, was attended by representatives from all the countries behind the Iron Curtain, except Russia. It looked as if this situation might be repeated at Amsterdam. But apparently the decision of the Russian Orthodox Church in Moscow not to participate in the Assembly binds also the Orthodox Churches in Bulgaria, Yugoslavia and Roumania.

during the first half of this year, we can see that the
Communist parties in power behind the Iron Curtain
have not repeated the mistakes of the early repressive
policy of the Bolsheviks. They start from the more
conciliatory attitude which at present characterizes the
relations of Church and State in the U.S.S.R.[1] Sur-
veying developments in the Balkans in 1947, Cmdr
Stephen King-Hall noted that there had been far less
political hostility to the Church than most people
expected. The Communist leaders had the wisdom
not to add to their difficulties by antagonizing the
Churches. In countries like Yugoslavia they have been
the more inclined to favour the Church and seek its
goodwill and support, because the Orthodox Church
has shared with them the trials and sacrifices imposed
by the German occupation. In the same way, Catholic
and Communist in France were for a time at least
drawn together because of common participation in
the resistance movement. The separation of Church
and State has become law in almost every country
where the Communists are in control. Thus in
Bulgaria, Article 78 of the Constitution ensures to all
citizens freedom of conscience and religion, as well as
freedom in carrying out religious rites. 'A special law
regulates the legal status, the material support and the
right of self-regulation and self-government of the
various religious communities.' In Yugoslavia, the

---

[1] It should, however, be noted that in its first year, Tito's
government arrested and executed or imprisoned many Catholic
priests, ostensibly for collaborating with Tito's enemies. The
charge may have been true in some cases, but the desire to
weaken the Church was the main ground of these proceedings.

separation of Church and State was accompanied by disendowment. The Church was deprived of nearly all its property in land, to facilitate agrarian reform. But these difficulties have brought inner renewal to the Orthodox Church. 'The Churches have never been so full as they are to-day. Church-goers give most generously to the support of the clergy.' Apparently the clergy are dependent on their congregations, as among Congregationalists and Baptists in this country. 'Daily services are held morning and evening in all the churches. There is no censorship on the preaching except from the church authorities themselves.' Self-sacrificing efforts are being made to maintain the Theological Faculty of the Orthodox Church in Belgrade, and the Faculty is still part of the University and still receives some support from the State, in spite of the separation of Church and State. It is noteworthy that though there is no official religious instruction in the public schools, religious instruction is permitted during free periods in the curriculum. Attendance is voluntary, and the teachers who give it receive payment from collections arranged by the Church, to which people give very generously. In this particular, clearly Yugoslavia is ahead of Russia. This also seems to be the case in regard to the Church's participation in social service. In Yugoslavia such participation is welcomed. The attitude of Tito's government towards church-life is described officially as one of interested concern.

While the first responsibility of the priests is in the realm of spiritual affairs, the government hopes that

Church leaders, particularly in the villages, will play an increasingly prominent role in the education of illiterates, in cultural activities, organizing co-operatives and in humanitarian works. The Churches have a very significant role and ought to perform it side by side with the government.

The Patriarch Gavrilo has urged the clergy throughout the country to support all activities for the benefit of the people sponsored by the government. Such co-operation between clergy and State-officials goes beyond anything reported as yet from Russia.

The Orthodox Church is a minor factor in Hungary, Czechoslovakia and Poland, and Communist governments have to deal with Roman Catholics and Protestants. In Poland, the vast majority of the people belong to the Roman Catholic Church, and in Hungary the peasants are mostly Catholic. In Czechoslovakia and Hungary, the Reformed Churches are vigorous. Both Catholics and Protestants have close links with the West, and with the exception of the Lutherans, who have too often been subservient to the State, both Catholics and Protestants have traditions of independence in regard to the State and refuse to surrender to the State their judgement on matters economic and political. It will not be so easy for Communist governments to come to terms with such Churches. The lines of policy hitherto followed have included the separation (more or less complete) of Church and State, the guarantee of religious freedom and religious equality, a careful avoidance of giving offence to the religious susceptibilities of workers and peasants, and measures to secure government control of the schools, while permitting religious instruction to continue generally on a voluntary basis. The position of the Churches in Poland perhaps exhibits Communist policy at its most generous. In present-day Poland, the Roman Catholics form 96 per cent of the population, leaving only 4 per cent associated with Orthodox and Protestant Churches. Yet now

The other Churches enjoy equal privileges with the Roman Catholic Church before the law, whereas before the war—in spite of the freedom of conscience anchored in the Polish Constitution of 1921—they did not receive recognition as organized church units. The State observes this innovation to the letter. In the Army there are now both Roman Catholic and Protestant chaplains.... The higher departments of State are keeping a careful watch to see that the religious minorities can preach their faith without restriction.

No doubt this jealous protection of religious equality is prompted in part by the desire to weaken the Roman Catholic Church. But clearly there is no prohibition of religious propaganda, such as that contained in the Russian Constitution of 1931, and the Œcumenical Council in Poland which embraces both the Orthodox and the Protestant Churches is able to undertake programmes of lectures addressed to the public. Then in Poland there has been up till now no complete separation of Church and State.

The Protestant Theological Faculty of the University of Warsaw is maintained entirely by the State. In the schools confessional religious instruction is compulsory. But the different confessions must support their own clergy financially and they only receive a small subsidy from the State for reconstruction of their damaged Church buildings.

In Hungary, Kingsley Martin when visiting the country last June (1948) observed that 'Until now the Party has taken every precaution to appease the Church.' He adds: 'Whether the Communists' tenderness for Catholic susceptibilities really reassures the Catholic peasantry, I doubt. In any case, the decision to nationalize the Catholic schools (in July) will undo the conciliatory effect of the policy of appeasement.' This decision has since been denounced by Cardinal Mindszenty, Prince Primate of Hungary.[1] The position of religious instruction in the schools in Hungary will be similar to that in Yugoslavia. The Reformed Churches are prepared to accept the new educational set-up and provide religious instruction on a voluntary basis. The Roman Church desires to retain its schools, or at least to have confessional religious instruction made compulsory as in Poland. The Communists hope to have the Protestants with them not only on this but on other issues. It is calculated that the separation of Church and State and the guarantees of religious liberty and equality will strengthen the other Churches, Reformed and Orthodox, and weaken the Roman Catholic Church. If the Reformed Church in Hungary would give unconditional support to the new state-system, it would be in a much more favourable position than the Roman Church.

[1] The situation in Hungary is the subject of an authoritative article in *The Times* of 29 July 1948.

The Government has sent the Reformed Church several attractive invitations to do this, but it has not answered. The Reformed Church has expressed its sincere approval of certain measures passed by the new Government, especially of the new land-reform law which affects the Church considerably. But it reserves the right to disapprove of certain other measures introduced by the State, if the case arises.

Karl Barth, from whose report these particulars are taken, adds:

I did not meet anyone in the Reformed Church who gave full allegiance and confidence to the new system. The childish enthusiasm of the fiery red Dean of Canterbury—who had visited Hungary shortly before I did—only aroused their amazement. The Reformed Church is in danger of not complying with the demands of the ruling party to make a decision—which would mean a decision in favour of that party.... The Reformed Church is also resisting the even closer and stronger temptation to join the Roman Catholics in forming a definite opposition. By doing so it could win many friends also.

The same issue arises in Czechoslovakia, and there the leaders of the Reformed Churches are divided on the question of their attitude towards the new Communist government, some being inclined to give it general approval and support, while others, perhaps the majority, would not go further than the line taken by the Reformed Church in Hungary. With regard to religious instruction in schools, the Czechoslovak School Ministry has outlined a proposed new school law which

will basically keep up the status of religious instruction in primary and secondary schools as heretofore. Pupils belonging to denominations recognized by the State, whose parents desire it, will receive religious instruction.[1] Text-books and other educational necessities for religious instruction will as before require the approval of the Church authorities. Details about the number of periods intended for religious instruction are left to the hands of the Government.

The general impression left by this survey will be that the Churches behind the Iron Curtain at the present moment enjoy a large measure of religious liberty, and in some instances the government's insistence on religious equality means that religious minorities are in a more favourable position than they were before. Thus the Jews in Roumania feel that they possess a social status and a security under the new régime, which were previously denied to them. But if Cmdr Stephen King-Hall is correctly informed, the attitude of Communists towards the Churches is already changing. He writes in his *News-Letter* (17 June 1948):

It is clear that the non-belligerent attitude of the Communists to the national churches immediately after the war was a piece of political window-dressing. At first, until the Communist régimes were firmly established, the Churches were not only tolerated but treated with patronage. As the Churches have emerged as centres of opposition to Communist tyranny, so Communist pressure has been increasing. All sorts of methods are being employed to curtail church activity, with the ultimate aim of completely eliminating Christianity and other forms of opposition to materialism.

[1] Actually, the new education law provides compulsory religious instruction in State schools for children from 6 to 16 years of age, unless parents object to such instruction.

It is noteworthy, however, that nearly all the examples he gives of Communist pressure are of pressure directed against the Roman Catholic Church which has declared its antagonism to the new régimes. The Communists can hardly be blamed for taking up the challenge. But it is also clear that the Communists are interested in the Churches only in so far as they can be used to further their policies. Actually both the Orthodox and the Reformed Churches, even while declining to become tools of the State, are useful agents for Communist propaganda. While then the Communists are naturally suspicious of any religious organizations which will not declare themselves unreservedly on their side, yet so long as such organizations are serviceable in any direction and in any degree, toleration and even patronage will still be extended to them.

The value of the spokesmen of the Churches as agents of Communist propaganda should not be overlooked or underrated. Pronouncements by Church authorities are the more useful, because the Churches retain some measure of independence and because they repeat Soviet propaganda in all sincerity, being for the most part unable to correct it so long as they are cut off from the West. Thus Archbishop Luka of the Crimea, writing in the *Journal* of the Moscow Patriarchate, appealed to Christians in 'Anglo-Saxon countries' to thwart 'the bloody plans of their militarists'. 'The Archbishop's plea...recalls the fate of such historical conquerors as Tamerlane, Alexander the Great, Napoleon and Hitler. He urged Western Christians to remember the lessons of the Bible and what happened to "pale Belshazzar," who saw the handwriting on the wall, and the Assyrians whom the Lord exterminated for attempting to capture Jerusalem.' Asserting that the United States are 'fearful of the inevitable approach of Socialism and Communism', Archbishop Luka declared that 'this fear is well founded, because if Communism did not enjoy the sympathy of millions, its enemies would have no need to reach for atom bombs'. Here the Soviet propaganda imputing aggressive intentions to the Western democracies is naïvely accepted and as naïvely repeated.[1] Similarly, a letter from a Czech correspondent which appeared in *The Friend* (18 June 1948) quite innocently observes that 'between the union of Slavonic countries and the union of Western countries, there is one main difference: the first was not made for military purposes, the second explicitly for them....I know that you look upon the foreign policy of the U.S.S.R. as imperialistic. Those who have for centuries made imperialistic policy simply cannot believe that any State in the world can follow other ends.' It is very easy for Christians behind the Iron Curtain to accept uncritically Soviet propaganda about the policy of the Western democracies. So long as they are content to echo it, not only may it strengthen the appeal of such propaganda abroad, but also in event of a break between East and West, the Churches

[1] A still more striking illustration of this endorsement of Soviet propaganda by the Orthodox Church is the reason given for declining the invitation to Amsterdam. They decline because 'the Œcumenical movement pursues in the main political, anti-democratic and non-ecclesiastical purposes'.

will stand for Slav unity and embrace the side of the
U.S.S.R. It is also worth noting that Christians unconsciously slide into Marxist grooves of thought.
Thus Archbishop Luka speaks of 'the *inevitable* approach of Socialism and Communism'. This idea
of 'inevitability' is a Marxist proposition, which
a Christian might counter with G. K. Chesterton's
question: 'Shall we abolish the inevitable?' Similarly
Dr Hromadka writes of 'some moral standards, social
conventions of decency, punctuality, politeness, personal correctness, honesty, decorativeness and refine-
ment' as 'precious values of bourgeois culture' which
unfortunately have to be sacrificed in the process of
revolution. This conception of *bourgeois* culture and
of tolerance and freedom as peculiar to it is again
a Marxist conception which ought not to command
Christian assent.

Does this acceptance of Marxist ways of thinking
point the road to accommodation and open the way
to an enduring partnership between the Churches and
the new Communist régimes? Leaders of the Russian
Orthodox Church profess themselves satisfied with
the present relations of Church and State in the
U.S.S.R. Thus Archbishop Luka says:

The Russian clergy live at full peace with the government because the latter has given the Church full freedom and does not interfere with its internal affairs....
Materialism, which is the ideological basis of Communism, is completely alien to the Orthodox Church,
but this does not prevent us from seeing all the good,
full of social truth, that the new state system has
brought us, and we welcome it with pure hearts.

Yet this very rejection of the ideological basis of Marxist Communism means that Church and government are by no means reconciled.

Officially religion is still regarded as a deplorable superstition and no churchgoer can ever hope to gain admittance to the Communist Party. The clergy on the other hand preach a spiritual faith which is fundamentally at odds with Marxist materialism; their very existence is a standing challenge to the doctrine that all wisdom and moral authority rest in the Party.[1]

In general the concessions made to religious institutions 'cannot be regarded as indicating any change in the official philosophy of the ruling party or any modification of its undiluted secularism of outlook and policy'.[2] The Marxist philosophy as expounded by Lenin and Stalin remains anti-Christian, and if the Communist government concedes certain liberties to the Church and forgoes the use of forcible methods of conversion, it is because it relies on its monopoly of education and on the hope of securing the full allegiance of youth. 'The young generation is, at least in its most lively and active representatives, growing up completely without any direct religious influence and education.'[3] The Communist youth organization, the Komsomol, sternly represses any weakening in opposition to religion on the part of youth. Towards the close of 1947, a discussion took place between the Soviet papers *Komsomol Truth* and *The Young Bolshevik*.

[1] John Fischer, op. cit. p. 101.
[2] P. A. Micklem, *The Sacred and the Secular*, p. 194.
[3] Dr Hromadka, *Christian News-Letter*.

The latter recommended that leniency be shown to believers and that they should be patiently taught how harmful religious faith is. The argument was settled by the Central Committee of the Komsomol: it decreed that Communists were prohibited to go to church. Their attitude toward religion—according to *Komsomol Truth*—is clear and unchangeable. It is considered inadmissible for members of the Komsomol to believe in God and to observe religious rites. The recommendation of *The Young Bolshevik* is called 'nothing but an effort to prove the possibility of a union of materialism with faith and idealism. That necessarily means leaving Marxism.' The committee recalled Stalin's statement that 'the Communist Party cannot be neutral to religion' and called for a continued 'offensive ideological struggle against religion'.

Tolerance is thus regarded as a deviation from Marxist orthodoxy. The government relies in the main on the place given to Marxism-Leninism in higher education. The interesting tables summarizing the curricula employed in medical and agricultural education, presented in Mr Eric Ashby's *Scientist in Russia*, reveal that medical students in the first two years of their course devote 250 hours to the study of Marxism-Leninism— 150 hours in lectures and 100 hours practical—the nature of the practical demonstrations is not explained by Mr Ashby. Budding agricultural experts devote 8 per cent of their time to Marxist philosophy and political economy.[1] So long as this indoctrination of youth is successful, the concession of liberties to the Church will not hinder the conversion of the people to the new religion. In the parallel with the Counter-

[1] Op. cit. pp. 88, 90, 91.

Reformation suggested earlier in this chapter, the influence exerted by the Jesuits through education was not mentioned. Yet here is the most striking parallel between the Communist Party and the Jesuit Order. And there is no doubt of the appeal of Communism to youth. Inside and outside Russia 'Communism has inspired and will inspire a vigorous body of young men and women with high ideals'. The Communist Party may well feel confident that the future belongs to it and not to the Church. Moreover, so long as the Orthodox Church approves the Soviet system and abstains from any prophetic word of criticism, accepting the plea of necessity to excuse the offences of the Communist Party against justice and humanity, it may be regarded as an ally rather than a centre of opposition. And the Church may feel tolerably secure in its liberties and, so long as it retains full liberty of worship, may await hopefully the re-awakening of these spiritual instincts of human nature which a materialist philosophy and economic well-being can never satisfy. If, however, there were further signs of religious revival and if the Communists are still bent on eliminating Christianity and substituting Marxism-Leninism, then the government can resort to all the weapons it now holds in reserve. Constitutional guarantees are subject to revision, especially when constitutions are of recent date. The State is the only employer and can vary conditions of employment to further its cultural aim. The Church is economically dependent on the State and open to pressure on that account. The old methods of persecution may at any time be revived, if it should seem expedient to the authorities. The Communist Party in the U.S.S.R. and elsewhere keeps a watchful eye on all leaders, and in the case of religious leaders, those who are capable and outspoken can be arrested and tried on trumped-up political charges before a people's court and condemned to death or imprisonment after a trial which is a travesty of justice, as happened in Yugoslavia in the case of Archbishop Stepinac. But so far as Russia is concerned, the present *détente* between Church and State may continue indefinitely. The grant of religious liberty is a matter of expediency, not a question of principle, for the Communist government. As such it is precarious, but unless the Party becomes disappointed with the progress of Marxist orthodoxy or suspicious of the growing strength of the Church, the argument from expediency will still suffice to maintain the measure of liberty which the Church enjoys.

As already indicated, where Communist régimes have to deal with Roman Catholics and Protestants, the case is altered. In Hungary, as we have noted, the Catholic Church is in opposition, while the Reformed Church, though refusing to join with the Catholics in opposition, will not declare itself simply on the side of the new régime. Karl Barth formed the impression that the Hungarian Reformed Protestants would not remain silent when they ought to speak.

But they see too clearly the mistakes made in the past, to rush to the opposite extreme now. And from the social side they are not open to reject Communism altogether. They realize the weakness of the West only too well, and do not wish to be forced . . . into becoming partisans of Western political ideas.

In a statement published on 10 April 1948, the Synodal Council of the Reformed Church of Hungary declares its willingness to co-operate with the new régime and approves many of its measures. It welcomes the steps taken to establish complete freedom of religion, and presses for 'the assurance of complete freedom as regards the joining of religious denominations'. It approves

the abolition of the system of large estates and the acquisition of land by the peasants and the administration of the large companies in the interests of greater social justice for every one, as consistent with the Holy Scriptures. Our Church gladly carries out the work entrusted to it by God in a society built up from the workers—industrial workers, peasants and intellectuals—and regards this society as one in which the truths of the Gospel may have a better chance of success, although it will not necessarily be free from the constant temptation due to human sin.

This last qualification is a mild rebuke to the self-righteousness and dogmatic self-confidence of the Communist parties and governments. In another paragraph, the Church gently but definitely dissociates itself from the brutality and injustice which accompany the Communist revolutions.

A revolutionary transformation of such vast proportions and elemental strength as the present one, cannot take place without much and great suffering. The Church would be disloyal to its Lord and to itself if it did not give proof of God's merciful love towards those who either through their own fault or through the faults of others are the victims of this great transformation. We must share their sufferings as the burden of the judgement on us all. While the Church carries out this Samaritan service, however, among these wounded souls, it must not allow itself to be forced into the position of having its holy service of mercy changed into political moves.

Thus, cautiously and courteously, the Reformed Church asserts its independence of judgement and action.

In the Russian Zone in Germany, the Lutheran Church refuses to become the tool and mouthpiece of the State. In a Whitsuntide Pastoral Letter, Bishop Dibelius insists on the importance of preserving the freedom to be sincere.

Everywhere where the State claims absolute power, it shows the sinister tendency of compelling people to be insincere. We are all familiar with this from the days of National Socialism. At that time millions of people were forced by threats and intimidation to say things which were really abhorrent to them....A tendency to mendaciousness came over the whole life of the German people. It undermined the morale and destroyed all true community. It destroyed the faith of innumerable Christians who could not stand up to the temptation....Times like these must never return. We Christians are responsible for seeing that they do not return. Let us take up the struggle against any pressure exerted upon our convictions and consciences. We should indeed obey the authorities in the external things of life, as long as they do not ask us to do something that is against God's commandment. But in cases where we have to express a conviction—in elections, in demonstrations, in deciding for a party, in plebiscites and on similar occasions, we are not called upon to be obedient: the only thing that matters then is our own conscientious conviction. Through this in God's name, we may preserve the freedom to be sincere.

A letter addressed to Marshal Sokolovski on 11 May by the Bishops and other Protestant leaders in the Eastern Zone of Germany expresses the spirit of this Whitsuntide Pastoral in three basic principles:

(1) According to Christian teaching, it is the duty of the individual Christian and never of the Church as a whole to obey the State authorities, unless they act contrary to God's commandments. But the Church is not allowed to make itself into an executive organ of State policy.

(2) If the Church has a message about political questions this message can only grow out of the inner compulsion of the Christian message.

(3) The freedom of the Church to take a positive or negative attitude toward political measures is an inalienable part of the religious freedom which the Church must request the State to give, and of which it already has been solemnly assured in the constitution of the provinces of the Eastern Zone.

In accordance with these principles, the Church requested Marshal Sokolovski to give instructions, that in future the Church should not be asked—either by the military government or by civilian authorities—to give any message concerning political questions: but to leave it to the Church to speak if and when it is called by God to speak about such questions. Neither in Hungary nor in the Eastern Zone of Germany is this independent attitude of the Churches palatable to the authorities. Indeed, the Communist must regard any claim to speak under God's direction either as delusion or as humbug and hypocrisy. In Hungary the broad-casting of religious services has been suspended, because the Churches are unwilling to submit sermons to State censorship. In the Eastern Zone, the *Pots-damer Kirche*, a Sunday newspaper in Brandenburg, was confiscated because it published a declaration from Church leaders which contained the following passage:

If anyone says 'yes', by giving his signature, he is saying 'yes' to the actual question before him, not to anything else. He has a right to protest against the misuse of his consent afterwards, in order to carry through certain measures at home or abroad which he did not mean to approve and to which he cannot give his assent. If anyone does *not* sign, this does not mean that he has said 'No' to German unity, nor that he should be branded as a traitor to his country.

The declaration was read in all the Churches in Germany on Trinity Sunday, without opposition. It is clear, however, that Communist authorities will hamper and restrict the Church in publishing its judge-ments, so long as those judgements are independent and displeasing to the authorities.

In Czechoslovakia, the Synodal Council of the Czech Brethren sent a message to Dr Gottwald, when he was Prime Minister, assuring him that the positive attitude of the Church towards creating a new and more just social order was unchanged. They offered the co-operation of the Church in educating a self-disciplined and responsible people on Christian principles. Many Church leaders and representative bodies urged their followers to vote for the new government in the farcical election which the Communists staged in May, thus falling short of the independent line taken by Bishop Dibelius and other German Protestants. But even those leaders who are most ready to see the good in the new régime and to identify themselves with it as far as possible, realize that the fundamental antagonism of Marxism to Christianity is not lightly to be overcome. Thus Dr Hromadka, who rightly deprecates carping criticism of the new régime and urges Christians to co-operate with it, is fully aware of the risks involved in such co-operation. He concludes his most impressive contribution to the *Christian News-Letter*, No. 311, in the following terms:

The era of liberal bourgeoisie with its indifference, neutrality and tolerant indulgence is over. The present rulers have a definite and aggressive *Weltanschauung*, even if they refrain from an attack upon the Church and religion. Our faith and Christianity will—humanly speaking—prevail only under two conditions: (1) that they carry their witness without trying to be a reservoir and stronghold of the old social and economic order, and (2) that they are really based on the realities of the prophetic and apostolic message and know what the Crucifixion and Resurrection of the Incarnate Word of God are. It will be a life-and-death struggle. If the Church becomes a real confessing Church, she will not only be a rallying point of all who have found a way out of confusion and despair, but she will save from material corruption the noble aspirations of the new order. It is a time of great perils as well as of great hopes.

We may note in conclusion that the relations of Church and State are not the same throughout the countries behind the Iron Curtain. In Russia, the State and the Churches have found a *modus vivendi* which may continue to be satisfactory to both parties for some time to come. In the satellite States, the relations are still taking shape. On the one hand, where the Roman Catholic Church is powerful, antagonism is avowed and open conflict inevitable. On the other, the Churches are given a share in the education of children and in social activities which is denied them in Russia. It is not irrelevant to observe that agrarian reforms in the countries of South-eastern Europe have not yet followed the Russian model. Such reforms have favoured the extension of peasant proprietorship. One would suppose that the Communist governments in Czechoslovakia and Yugoslavia, for example, may be aware that the true model for them to follow should be found in the Danish form of agricultural co-operatives, not in the Russian collectives. The future of religious liberty behind the Iron Curtain will depend on whether Russia and the Cominform insist on all satellite states following the Russian model in education and agriculture. This policy if ruthlessly and fanatically pursued and enforced will almost certainly fail. It will force all the Churches into opposition and expose them to severe persecution, such as the Confessional Church had to endure under the Nazis. It will provoke resistance on the part of the peasantry, and be even more disastrous than the brutal liquidation of the Kulaks was in Russia. It will rouse national feeling among Czechs, Poles and Hungarians which will be directed against Russian tyranny. The governments may not cease to be Communist, but Communism will develop in differing national forms. It is not impossible that from such a conflict, Christian Socialists may supplant the Communists as the directing power. In any case we are witnessing and we are involved in a conflict of religions in the twentieth century, and the only hope of resolving it without resort to force is to pledge governments to respect religious liberty.

SUPPLEMENTARY NOTE.

Since this chapter was written, the Lutheran Bishop Ordas and Cardinal Mindszenty in Hungary have been tried and condemned on charges of currency-offences, of espionage and treason. In Bulgaria, fifteen Evangelical pastors have been sentenced to various terms of imprisonment on similar offences. They may have been technically guilty of espionage and treason, as defined in the laws of Hungary and Bulgaria, but the judicial procedure offends against article 11, and the laws offend against article 19 of the Declaration of Human Rights adopted at Paris. [See Appendix II for the text of these articles]. These trials are not acts of justice, but acts of war. They are intended to discredit Christian leaders and break all their connections with the West. They are moves in the cold war for which Soviet policy is mainly and directly responsible.

Chapter V

THE FAILURE OF LEFT-WING INTELLECTUALS

There is an intimate connexion between religious liberty and Liberal democracy. The effective maintenance of religious liberty is a necessity for the creation and preservation of Liberal democracy. The surrender or disparagement of Liberal democracy tends to undermine religious liberty. Democracy is not just a device for settling national policy by counting heads instead of breaking them. It is not a simple agreement to abide by majority decisions. A democracy with any pretentions to be called Liberal must ensure that minorities are heard and considered, and that the judicature is not overruled by the executive. In short, it must establish constitutional liberties for minorities and individuals.

If Professor Harold Laski's judgement is to be trusted, the traditions and practice of Liberal democracy have been gravely imperilled by the threat of sabotage from the Right. Capitalists and believers in capitalism are losing faith in Liberal democracy because the advance of democratic Socialism imperils the principles of the system and the privileges of those who profit by it.

Even Great Britain and the United States, where the Liberal tradition is most strongly rooted, find in their midst profound suspicions of democracy because, as their ability to penetrate new markets declines, the threat of democracy to economic privilege becomes ever more manifest....It is peculiarly significant that in Great Britain, the main attack upon democracy, especially in the economic realm, has come from men who in the last sixty or seventy years have been trained in imperialist habits of thought by Indian experience.[1]

A class which threatens, let alone attempts, constitutional sabotage when the verdict of democracy goes against it invites that suspicion of the democratic process which is fatal to most of the spiritual gains of civilized life.[2]

The thesis of Professor Laski's book, *The State in Theory and Practice*, was that the main threat to Liberal democracy in this country would come from the Right.

The habits of tolerance, which are the mark of a system which feels secure, no longer win the favour which was widespread a generation ago. Faith in the power of reason to settle controversies with justice no longer awakens the same response as in the nineteenth century: ideas hasten to clothe themselves in arms for fear lest their own virtue be too unsubstantial to prevail.[3]

Professor Laski seems to have been much influenced by the Tory defence of the Lords' veto and by the now almost forgotten challenge of events at the Curragh. He was sure that no far-reaching programme extending public ownership and limiting private ownership of

---

[1] *The State in Theory and Practice*, p. 263.
[2] Op. cit. p. 217.   [3] Op. cit. p. 309.

the means of production would be put through Parliament without the Conservatives resorting to constitutional sabotage. Nothing like that has happened, and Professor Laski must either believe that the programme is not revolutionary enough or that the State in Marxist theory is not the State in British practice. Even at the time he was writing, it was ludicrously untrue to suggest, as he did, that the main attack on democracy came from imperialist proconsuls. Suspicion of democracy, contempt for democracy, were being fostered by our left-wing intellectuals, H. G. Wells and G. Bernard Shaw. The discrediting and destruction of Liberal democracy have been the work of impatient planners and violent revolutionaries. Professor Laski's analysis of Fascism is vitiated by the fact that he treats it throughout as a capitalist reaction to constitutional change when it was in fact a reaction to violent revolution. The repudiation of Liberal democracy came first from the Communist left, which did not and does not hesitate to suspend the democratic process in a manner fatal to most of the spiritual gains of civilized life, since such spiritual gains are regarded either as bourgeois prejudices or at best as luxuries only permissible when available to all in a time of economic security.

By accepting uncritically Marx's faulty economic analysis of the so-called capitalist system, by adopting the Marxist theory of class-war and the associated view of the State as in its essence and nature the instrument of class-domination, Professor Laski has done more to undermine the spiritual gains of civilized life than all the Diehard Tories in England. Like the Webbs, he exaggerated the benefits and excused the excesses of the Russian Revolution. Like the Webbs, he belittled every value enshrined in the British tradition of Liberal democracy. Habeas Corpus and the Bill of Rights, the independence of the judicature, the principle that the accused is to be regarded as innocent until proved guilty, in short all the safeguards of individual liberty are represented as conceived in the interests of capitalists and only likely to be maintained so long as it suits the interests of capitalists. Liberty of thought, indeed all our civil liberties, are assumed to be effective only for the economically independent and a handful of intellectuals.

The chance to think freely has always been a function of economic independence: and a Society which associates economic independence with the ownership of property is, in fact, limiting freedom of thought, for all save a small minority of its members, to the owners of property. So long as a workman can be dismissed, not because he is inefficient, but because his economic or political opinions arouse distrust in his employer, their relations impose constraints upon the former which are likely to be fatal to his freedom. That is why freedom of opinion under capitalism has always seemed less real to the working-classes than it has to the employer or to the intellectual.[1]

The Webbs develop the same argument at length in *Soviet Communism* (vol. II, pp. 1025 *et seq.*). Western freedom is freedom only for the rich. They anticipate that to the educated intellectual of the Western world

[1] *The State in Theory and Practice*, p. 210.

their argument will appear mere sophistry.[1] It is not only to the educated intellectual but to the intelligent trade unionist or co-operator that the argument will appear to be mere sophistry. It is simply not true that effective liberty of thought and expression is confined to a small minority of British citizens. When we have recognized to the full that wage-earners, under capitalism, were subjected in the past, and in a rapidly diminishing degree still are subjected to economic and social pressures restricting their freedom, it yet remains true that religious liberty, though bought with a price, has been a reality for the workers, and the secrecy of the ballot has been a defence against those pressures in the political sphere which would be fatal to the workers' freedom. When things were at the worst, let us say, in the days of the Tolpuddle Martyrs, it was not true of the British workers that they had nothing to lose but their chains. To suggest that their civil and other liberties to-day are ineffective and illusory is sophistry. It is not in Great Britain, but in every Communist-dominated country that workmen can be and are constantly being dismissed, because their economic or political opinions arouse distrust in their employer. Where the State is the only employer, the relations between employer and employed are more than likely to be fatal to the latter's freedom. Moreover, if the situation in the West were as black as Professor Laski and the Webbs assumed, if liberty of thought were effective only for a handful of intellectuals, it is to the interest of the workers that that

[1] *Soviet Communism*, p. 1033.

freedom should be maintained inviolate. It is to the interest of the workers that Professor Laski remains at liberty to say and write what he thinks and is not compelled to toe the party line. The Communist dictatorships, like the Fascist, undermine intellectual sincerity and integrity, and this is never to the advantage of the common man. Professor Laski notes, apparently with regret, that habits of tolerance are losing ground and that faith in the power of reason to settle controversies with justice no longer awakens the old response. 'Ideas hasten to clothe themselves in arms for fear lest their own virtue be too unsubstantial to prevail.' He has the Fascists in mind, but the first offenders and the real culprits are the Communists, and in large measure Professor Laski has endorsed their philosophy. It is the Communist philosophy which assumes that there is no moral principle at stake in the practice of toleration. Habits of tolerance, as Professor Laski following Marx assumes, are the mark of a system which feels secure. It is the Communist philosophy adopted by Professor Laski which assumes that there are no principles of justice to which reason can appeal in settlement of controversies. Like other Marxists, he indignantly denies the interpretation of historic materialism as economic determinism. Marxism pays lip-service to the existence of other factors beside the economic factor. But in his analysis, Professor Laski, like other Marxists, treats these other factors as practically negligible, and he does not recognize ultimate moral right as an independent factor. There is no independent criterion of justice. Each class is entitled to determine its own claims and to regard the satisfaction of these claims as justice.[1] Since each class identifies justice with the realization of its economic interests, justice means one thing to a property-owner and another to the wage-earner. The issue will be decided not by reason, but by economic pressure and if necessary by physical violence. The conflicting parties will struggle to secure control of the State to enforce their own idea of justice. In view of his repudiation of any objective standard of justice it is difficult to see why Professor Laski embraces the side of the workers. By accepting the Marxist analysis he has himself destroyed the ethical basis of tolerance and of the appeal to reason, and encouraged the resort to brute force. The extent of his surrender to Marxism can be gauged by his review of the growth of the social-service State in Great Britain.[2] You might well suppose that on such a review he would admit himself convicted of rhetorical exaggeration in regarding the State simply as the instrument of class-domination. But no, this phase of social history does not reveal to Professor Laski the operation of a social conscience acting as arbiter between the conflicting claims of different classes. 'What we call, in fact, the growth of a social conscience is simply the changed idea of established expectation which has been brought about by the class-struggle.' 'All the gains have had to be fought for grimly by

[1] 'Each of us makes his own right or wrong in politics: they grow out of the experience in which we find ourselves immersed.' Op. cit. p. 212.

[2] Op. cit. pp. 169 ff.

those upon whom they conferred benefit.[1] As a matter
of fact not all the gains have been fought for grimly by
those upon whom they conferred benefit. In no case
did prospective beneficiaries fight alone, and those who
fought for them and with them and often took the
initiative did so not because they wanted to be on the
winning side, but because they believed the cause to
be just. The changed idea of established expectation
—a very inadequate definition of the social conscience,
by the way—was not brought about by the class-
struggle. This growth of the social conscience determined the character and issue of the class-struggle in
each case. Professor Laski's thesis is nothing but a
repetition of the foolish Marxist antithesis, to the effect
that life determines consciousness and not vice versa.
From this starting-point it is not possible to understand the growth of the social conscience. Because it
is necessarily related to and concerned with the class-
struggle, Laski assumes that it is generated by it. If it
were, it would not be a social conscience. For the
same reason he fails to appreciate the Idealist Theory
of the State, which has probably contributed more
to the growth of the social conscience and the development of the social-service State than has the
class-struggle, and certainly more than the Marxist
misinterpretation of the class-struggle.

In the end Professor Laski is left without any con-
vincing ethical principle on which to base his adherence to constitutional methods of reform or by
which to justify his appreciation of the spiritual gains

[1] P. 172.

of civilized life. Here is his half-hearted adhesion to Liberal democracy.

Where the members of a State enjoy fundamental political rights in a degree real enough to make effectively possible the transformation of dissent into orthodoxy, I believe that it is the duty of the citizen to exhaust the means placed at his disposal by the constitution of the State before resorting to revolution.[1] I admit that the nature of capitalist democracy weights the scales unduly against him. I admit also that this is a counsel of prudent expediency rather than of ultimate moral right. But I believe that the gains which are inherent in the technique of constitutionalism are profounder, even though they are more slow, than those which are implicit in the revolutionary alternative.[2]

It is apparent also that Professor Laski would approach the question of compensation to dispossessed property-owners in the same spirit. He would not object in principle to the Communist policy of dispossessing property-owners without any compensation whatever. Indeed, if there was no other way of satisfying the expectations of the workers, he would regard it as just. Presumably like Professor G. D. H. Cole he would approve a modest measure of compensation, but he would admit that this is a counsel of prudent expediency rather than of ultimate moral right. Clearly Professor Laski's faith in constitutional methods has no secure foundation. He is not to be

[1] Since Professor Laski grounds his adhesion to the Labour Party on his conviction that this is the actual situation in Great Britain, he is clearly convicted of rhetorical exaggeration in asserting that freedom of thought is effective only for property-owners and intellectuals.   [2] P. 213.

trusted as a defender of either Liberal democracy or religious liberty.

Far and away the worst offender is the veteran socialist advocate, G. Bernard Shaw. Perhaps it is no longer necessary to take Shaw seriously, and yet one is reluctant to think of a writer so vital and so challenging as becoming a spent force. But I confess the prefaces to *Too True to be Good* and *On the Rocks* make me feel that Shaw of all people has deserted to the enemy in time of crisis. I find myself echoing a couplet from one of Lowell's sonnets on reading Wordsworth's sonnets in defence of capital punishment.

> And always 'tis the saddest sight to see
> An old man faithless in Humanity.

For when Shaw declares that dictatorship like Guinness is good for us, and derides as nonsense the idea of every normal adult sharing in the responsibility of government, he is 'an old man faithless in Humanity'. The same is true when he lines up with Wordsworth in defence of capital punishment. No doubt it was difficult for Shaw to resist the temptation to address to G. K. Chesterton a legitimate *argumentum ad hominem*; to point out the parallel between the Communist system and the medieval Church system. But to acclaim this as the right system of government and to declare that the trouble with the Church system was neither its authoritarianism nor its methods, but its mistaken choice of heretics, is surely indefensible. Now that the Communists have branded belief in the institution of private property as the only serious

modern heresy, and the possession of private property
as the only serious modern crime, Mr Shaw would
have us acknowledge the wisdom and applaud the
policies of Comrade Stalin. Not only the revival of the
Inquisition but also the liquidation of all who are
thought to be socially incompatible apparently wins
Mr Shaw's hearty approval.

The preface to *On the Rocks* is devoted to the defence
of a paradox. It opens with a denial of the sacredness
of human life, and it ends with an assertion of the
sacredness of criticism. Man has no right to live, but
he has a right to say freely what he thinks. One can
understand that Mr Shaw does not consider it worth
while to live without talking, but it will puzzle even
his genius to talk without living. However, since he is
always ready to straighten things out for the muddle-
headed bourgeois, he will explain no doubt in a future
preface how a man is to enjoy the right of criticism
while deprived of the right to live. In the meantime, he
argues on the one hand that society must exercise the
right to exterminate because there is a distinct criminal
class consisting of untamable persons of a ferocious
and unscrupulous character, and on the other that
society must respect the right to criticize because it is
so difficult, indeed next to impossible, to distinguish
the true critic and pioneer from the criminal or lunatic.
His solution of the problem he has thus posed is to
suggest that the critic be immune so long as he only
talks or writes plays. Once the critic acts on his un-
popular opinions, he may lawfully be exterminated as
a criminal or a lunatic. This common-sense suggestion,

already acted on in modern society, has some practical utility, but it is obviously no solution of the problem. Criticism when it is merely talk divorced from action will always be irresponsible, and will be the less deserving of respect and attention precisely because it is irresponsible. On the other hand, if you once grant to governments the right to exterminate, the right will be exercised against dangerous opinions as well as against dangerous actions, and no logical resistance to such extension is possible. Mr Shaw's defence of the right to exterminate renders absolutely futile his closing plea for toleration.

Mr Shaw is putting his trust in tolerant dictators. His friends and admirers underline the adjective, but it is the noun that matters. The distinctive feature of the prefaces is the advocacy of dictatorship. Mr Shaw believes in dictators, efficient ruthless dictators who mean to govern, but he hopes they will leave the individual his last great right, the right to grouse. To me this seems a pitiable surrender of a great mind to the reactionary currents of the present age. Mr Shaw has ceased to swim against the tide.

The right to exterminate!—One would have supposed that a true prophet would either denounce the right altogether or plead for its progressive circumscription until it falls into desuetude. In this country we have steadily restricted the use of this right by the State, and to-day we retain capital punishment in effect only for the crime of murder. In this regard England lags behind some modern States, but the grounds for the abolition of capital punishment are being more widely appreciated to-day. Such abolition should be our next great penal reform. But if the cause in whose service Roy Calvert laboured is to succeed, it must succeed in spite of Mr Shaw. To his mind the alternatives are either 'to disable the murderer once for all by making an end of him, or else waste the lives of useful and harmless people in seeing that he does no mischief and caging him cruelly like a lion in a show'. The first alternative seems obviously preferable to Mr Shaw: it is not in the least obvious to me, even on Mr Shaw's own premisses. Any force there may be in his contention depends on the assumption that some criminals are known to be incorrigible.

The real necessity arises only in dealing with untamable persons who are constitutionally unable to restrain their violent or acquisitive impulses, and have no compunction about sacrificing others to their own immediate convenience.

In criminology Mr Shaw seems to have got as far as Lombroso. It is very doubtful whether this real necessity arises anywhere save in Mr Shaw's imagination, and even if there are criminals who seem incorrigible in the present stage of our knowledge and faith, they should be kept alive in order that psychologists and moralists may perfect their respective wisdoms. Society has no right to exterminate homicidal maniacs, nor is it common sense to do so.

If the preface to *On the Rocks* merely repeated shoddy arguments in favour of capital punishment, it would not deserve serious attention. But Mr Shaw is not content to appear as a diehard in defence of our existing criminal code; he insists on the political necessity of killing, and advocates a more extensive use of the right to exterminate. His plea for capital punishment is nonsense: his demand for a more extensive use of the right to exterminate is dangerous nonsense. He starts from the position that the modern State must have a standard faith and a generally accepted ideal, and that it must have the power to get rid of those who do not accept this faith and who will not work for this ideal. This means that governments have the right to exterminate all who exhibit 'incorrigible social incompatibility'. In plain English, the party which can secure control of the government machine has the right to kill off its political opponents. Mr Shaw means this or he means nothing, and the concession of any such right means the betrayal of any civilization worthy of the name. Mr Shaw is furthering the triumph of barbarism.

What dictator or what tyrant would not be glad to be permitted to exterminate on the ground of 'incorrigible social incompatibility', when he himself is to be judge alike of incompatibility and incorrigibility? He is presented with a blank cheque to fill in exactly as he likes. Any champion of constitutional liberties will be aghast at such a proposal, and even the reformer in a hurry might be expected to think twice before claiming or conceding a right so indefinite. Mr Shaw has of course the courage of his convictions. The indefiniteness which damns the proposal in the eyes of anyone who values personal liberty is one of its attractions in the eyes of Mr Shaw. A wholesome terror may be inspired in the bosom of the individual citizen by the very fact that he does not know whether his existence is socially justified or not. The English are accustomed to living under a government whose claims upon them are strictly defined, and Mr Shaw thinks it would do us good to live under a régime of unlimited liability in morals. He thinks absolute powers of life and death may safely be entrusted to an institution like the O.G.P.U. 'The security against abuse of this power of life and death was that the Cheka had no interest in liquidating anybody who could be made publicly useful, all its interests being in the opposite direction.' Such a statement is either very innocent or very disingenuous. Either Mr Shaw does not know what he is talking about or he is talking with his tongue in his cheek. Actually, one may suspect, it is a case of fifty-fifty. Englishmen will never be such fools as to surrender their constitutional safeguards of life and liberty for the worthless security which apparently satisfies Mr Shaw.

The arguments by which Mr Shaw supports his thesis are as astonishing as the thesis itself. They amount to this. All through history, men have been exterminating political opponents. Though all previous attempts to exercise the right have missed the point, i.e. in each case the wrong people have been exterminated, yet the constant exercise of the right, throughout history, shows it to be necessary, and at last the Russians have found out the true criminal class which must be exterminated, namely the incurably acquisitive. Unfortunately the Russians, though theoretically sound, have proceeded to kill off intellectuals and Kulaks whose services to society are indispensable. Unfortunately also, they have done this, in spite of the security against abuse of the right in which Mr Shaw has such childlike confidence. The Russian experiment in extermination was at least aimed in the right direction, but hundreds and thousands of innocent and potentially useful citizens perished along with the criminal class. Ciliga calculates that of the peasants exterminated or exiled in 1932 not more than one-fifth were genuine Kulaks. The wisdom of dealing with the criminal class in this manner does not exactly leap to the eye.

If you are not satisfied with Mr Shaw's hasty review of history, and if you do not share his admiration for the extension of social responsibility at present in vogue in Russia, he has still a *tu quoque* argument up his sleeve. Private property in capital, particularly in land, confers on private individuals the right to exterminate. Such a right ought to be exercised by the State only. Mr Shaw is aware of the equivocation in his argument. The Highland landlord may exterminate crofters in the sense of turning them off his land. If this involves hardship and the danger of starvation for the crofters, this is tantamount to killing them, and the entire responsibility is held to lie at the door of the landlord. The sheer dishonesty of such an argument does not need formal exposure. In any case, the suggested parallel between abuses incidental to the private owner-ship of capital on the one side, and the deliberate activities of the Cheka in Russia or of Himmler in Germany on the other, halts pretty badly, and if it were exact, it is difficult to see how the abuses of capitalism can be erected into rational political principles in the new social order. And once again if Mr Shaw's preface means anything, it means precisely that. What is done unconsciously or half-consciously by individuals under capitalism, i.e. the extermination of those who cannot fit into the existing social order, should be done deliberately by politically responsible authorities in the Socialist commonwealth.

If we ask how Mr Shaw comes to advance with apparent conviction arguments so inadequate and indeed so sophistical for a thesis so dubious, part of the answer may lie in the fact that he is an Irishman. In one of George A. Birmingham's novels, *Found Money*, the cook at the vicarage, a Mrs Hegarty, informs the narrator of a conflict which is impending between Free State troops and members of the Irish Republican Army.

'And nobody'll be sorry for them when they are dead,' she went on, 'for it's what they deserve.' I had not the slightest idea what Mrs Hegarty's political sympathies were. She might for all I know be a Free Stater, a Republican, a Bolshevik, or even a Loyalist. Nor did I want to find out. The political principles of every Irish party seem to boil down to the same thing in the end. They all believe that the only hope of the country lies in the slaughter of most of its inhabitants. They differ, of course, about who are to constitute the minority which is to be allowed to survive.

This amiable belief Mr Shaw appears to share with his fellow-countrymen, and it probably accounts for his eager assertion of the right to exterminate. Mr Shaw is just a typical Irish party!

In Mr Shaw's own view he is exhibiting, not the unregenerate Irishman's belief in the political necessity of killing, but the true Irishman's clear-headed insight into the logic of the situation. The modern State must have a faith and must maintain its faith and its unity in the same way in which the medieval Catholic Church sought to achieve the same object, to wit, by exterminating heretics or the socially incompatible. Mr Shaw thinks this necessity inheres in the situation of the modern State whatever faith it adopts. It does not occur to him that the necessity may attach more particularly to the faith which he himself hopes the modern State will adopt, and that the assumed necessity follows from the defects and errors of his own creed. It is easy to see that Mr Shaw's desire to enforce his creed leads him to favour the right to kill. And not merely does his desire to enforce his creed determine the argument of the prefaces, but the cardinal points of his creed support and justify his faith in the necessity of forcibly suppressing heresy.

Of the three main articles of his faith, vegetarianism, the economics of Socialism, and creative evolution, the first does not call for comment unless indeed we may take comfort from the fact that Mr Shaw, though he still believes in the hangman, is not yet prepared to revert to cannibalism. We might have expected him to argue that since our right to live depends on our being useful to society, criminals who are useless when living should be made of some use when dead. Happily Mr Shaw, even when in the full tide of reaction, draws the line somewhere. But the economics of Socialism and the religion of creative evolution directly bear on his advocacy of the right to kill. Belief in the economics of Socialism means simply that Mr Shaw is a dogmatic collectivist. In regard to the institution of private property, Mr Shaw has sunk into what John Stuart Mill used to call 'the deep slumber of a decided opinion'. Unfortunately he talks and talks wildly in his sleep. 'The modern priesthood (the rulers in the modern State) must utterly renounce, abjure, abhor, abominate and annihilate private property as the very worst of all the devil's inventions for the demoralization of mankind.' A man who writes like this is no longer thinking: he is simply labouring under an obsession. No one at this time of day is going to deny the serious abuses of private ownership or to champion the unrestricted rights of private property: but that is no reason why an intelligent person should ignore the positive values associated with private property, or turn a blind eye to the equal dangers of demoralization and damnation under out-and-out collectivism in the totalitarian State. The Gospel warns us against the dangers of wealth, whether privately or collectively owned, and the history of monastic orders affords sufficient proof that the abolition of private property will not of itself save a community from corruption by wealth. If Mr Shaw really thinks private property the worst of all the devil's inventions, he must be very ignorant of Satan's devices.

A dogmatic collectivist is one who has not only stopped thinking on his *idée fixe* but who is also so sure of it that he is prepared to sacrifice his fellow men and women to its realization. Hence the wide use of the right to exterminate by fanatical Marxists in Russia and hence Mr Shaw's applause of their action. It is not strange if others think such dogmatists should themselves be exterminated, or if others propose to use the same right to enforce other dogmas. Mr Shaw's prefaces are essays in defence of Bolshevism. The defence serves only to arm their opponents. His argument plays right into the hands of the Fascists or indeed of any other group which has a social ideal it would like to enforce and which can secure power.

Of even greater interest is the connexion which Mr Shaw traces between the right to kill and the first article in his creed, the religion of creative evolution. This religion, it seems, undermines the sense of the sacredness of the individual life, and it does this in two ways. First 'the mystic distinction between Man and Brute vanishes'. Mr Shaw, as a vegetarian, might have deduced from this that it is as wrong to take the life of a brute as to take the life of a fellow-man. He draws the opposite conclusion. It is as right and as necessary to take the lives of our fellow-men, if they are a nuisance to us, as it is to take the lives of venomous or ferocious animals. The argument is worthless. Mr Shaw may deny any *mystic* distinction between Man and Brute, but he can hardly deny a distinction. Our right to take animal life is based on that distinction, and no set or race of men can claim in regard to their fellow-men the same sort of superiority as all men claim in regard to the animal creation, nor can any differences that exist between men be used to justify the right to commit the crime of murder.

The second way in which the religion of creative

evolution undermines the sacredness of human life is that it regards the individual merely as a link between generations, and never as an end in himself. This is involved in the denial of the immortality of the human soul, to which denial Mr Shaw seems to be committed. Anyway, if you believe in creative evolution, you think of individuals merely as means to social ends, or to the accomplishment of the purposes of the life-force. As no one knows what the purposes of the life-force are, such purposes may be conveniently identified with purposes that appeal to one's self. Having reached this point, the believer in the life-force easily merges into Mr Shaw's criminal class and finds that he has no compunction about sacrificing others if not to his own immediate convenience, at least to his own ultimate ideals.

Happily there are truer and better faiths available for mankind. It is possible for Society to believe not in the life-force but in the God and Father of our Lord Jesus Christ, and it is possible for Society to believe not in the economics of Socialism, which means distorting the facts and principles of economics and degrading the ideals of Socialism, but in scientific inquiry in economics as in other departments of knowledge, and in a genuinely co-operative commonwealth, not to be realized by the domination of any class or any dogmatic clique. But the trend of Mr Shaw's creed is unmistakable. The religion of creative evolution as he understands it is not an enlightened up-to-date faith: it is a degrading idolatry. Mr Shaw's religion has landed him on the rocks.

CHAPTER VI

THE RESPONSIBILITIES OF THE
CHRISTIAN CHURCH

WHAT standards should the Christian Church ask the civil power to maintain in things sacred? In this connexion, I use the term 'The Christian Church' to include any organized body of professing Christians which claims either to be the only legitimate representative of the true Church of Christ or to belong as one member among others to the body of Christ. The Roman Catholic Church which alone effectively and impressively makes the first of these claims is no doubt in a unique position and therefore carries unique responsibilities for the defence of religious liberty. But it is legitimate to assume that any Church claiming to be Christian will be bound by some at least of the same guiding principles. So it is legitimate to ask: What standards should the Christian Church ask the civil power to maintain in things sacred? We must raise the further question: Should the Christian Church invoke the aid of the civil power to discourage or stifle heretical, or non-Christian, or anti-Christian propaganda? Should the Christian Church accept privilege, i.e. establishment and endowment, from the civil power?

In a recent essay, Professor John Laird drew attention to the admirable discussion of this theme in the now neglected works of Isaac Watts. Dr Watts wrote

a short treatise on Civil Power in Things Sacred
(*Collected Works*, vol. IV), in which he said:

In the peculiarities of Christianity, I find nothing
that can be required or imposed by civil authority,
without entrenching on the rights and liberties of
mankind, and I was not willing to indulge anything
to be imposed upon heathen subjects by Christian
governors, which may not also be counted reasonable
and lawful for a heathen governor to impose upon
Christians.

On this, Professor Laird commented: 'It would not
be easy to find a fairer or more useful touchstone,
and Watts employed it with the most painstaking
scrupulousness.' As one example of painstaking
scrupulousness, we may cite his answer to the question,
whether the belief and profession of the one true God
should be imposed on all the nation under any penalty?
'I rather think it should not, and for these three
reasons: (1) Heathens may be useful members of the
State; (2) Penalties may make dissemblers and hypocrites, but good Christians are not to be made this way;
(3) A supreme governor, Socinian, Turk, or Deist,
may as legitimately penalize Athanasians.' For the
Christian Church to seek the aid of the civil power in
persecuting or suppressing heresies or non-Christian
religions, Dr Watts held to be sin. 'No religion hath
a right to be tolerated which professes and maintains
the persecution of other religions.' With regard to
more positive support by the civil power, Dr Watts
seems to have thought that some substratum of natural
religion might be encouraged by State action. Perhaps

the preachers of natural religion should be supported
by the State. If Dr Watts had had his way, the State
might have anticipated Lord Gifford's generous
endowment of natural theology! He was prepared
to countenance enforced instruction in the Law of
Nature. 'Compulsory attendance at lectures, explain-
ing laws and moral duties, if at reasonable times, is not
an infringement of true liberty.' But he would not go
as far as Locke was prepared to go in the constitution
he drew up for Carolina, and enforce attendance at
worship as well as at lectures. 'Compulsory attendance
at public worship, in terms of a sort of natural religion,
which is the foundation of all true revealed religion is
to be deprecated, in spite of Locke, Laws of Carolina,
Art. 95.' Dr Watts could see no justification for
establishment. It is the establishment of some one
Church by the civil power, 'which has fixed so many
wicked and mischievous religions throughout the
world and which hath excluded the only true religion
of Christ and the New Testament out of most of the
nations of the earth in former and later ages'. The
Christian Church should not accept privileges from
Christian governors, which it would not wish heathen
religions to receive from non-Christian governors.
Two principles emerge here which are binding on the
Christian Church. First, the Christian Church both in
her own conduct and in the conduct she would have
the civil power pursue is bound by the Golden Rule,
and second, if she believes in some form of the Law of
Nature, which requires the State to ensure certain
rights to men as such, then the Church must not only

claim such rights and liberties for her own members and for herself as a corporate body, but must also insist that the State conforms to such Law of Nature in dealing with all its subjects. The weakness and the failure of the Christian Church have been that she has too often been content to assert principles in defence of her own interests and too seldom been jealous for the rights of others.

The eminently fair and useful touchstone which Dr Watts employed so scrupulously, may not be susceptible of easy application in every concrete historical situation. A Church may be so intimately bound up with the life of a nation that she cannot simply decline the privilege of State recognition. Such is the position of the Presbyterian Church in Scotland, the Anglican Church in England, the Lutheran Church in the Scandinavian countries, the Reformed Church in Holland, the Orthodox Church in Greece, and the Roman Catholic Church in Italy or Spain. But where a Church accepts or retains a privileged position, it behoves her to be very jealous for the rights and liberties of religious minorities. In the realm of education, which as we have seen, must be either the meeting-place or the battlefield for Church and State in the modern world, co-operation with the State is desirable if it is possible, and such co-operation may involve State support of the Church in religious education. It would seem that any particular Church which accepts such State support should take her stand on the principle of concurrent endowment. It is perhaps hardly necessary to add that the Church should be scrupulously careful to safeguard the sincerity and intellectual integrity of the teaching profession.

In Great Britain, where broadcasting is entrusted to a public corporation, it may be questioned whether freedom of worship and freedom of thought have been adequately secured, and whether some responsibility does not rest on the Christian Church to influence the B.B.C. in the direction of providing opportunity for a still greater variety of expression of religious thought and thought about religion. The record of the B.B.C. is a fine one, alike in maintaining high standards of fairness, accuracy and courtesy in the broadcasts of its own staff, and in securing a fair representation of the main currents of faith and thought in this country. It also casts its net wide to bring to the microphone a judicious selection of individual expert opinion. But it may be questioned whether it provides sufficient opportunity for some clearly defined minorities to make themselves heard, whether in politics or religion. In politics, it might be in the interests of freedom if we heard more frequently from Communists and fellow-travellers. It would also be an advantage if party political broadcasts were more frequently supplemented by contributions from the cross-bench mind. That despised creature, the political mugwump, ought to have his turn at the microphone. There must be a widespread suspicion in the public mind at the present time that the logic of the situation points to the formation of a new coalition government, but this point of view has little chance of getting on the air, while party political broadcasts are the order of the day. In the sphere of religion, the very excellence of the present arrangements for religious broadcasting may blind us to some defects. The present arrangements provide admirably for the expression of the main currents of religious life and thought in this country both in periods of worship and hymn-singing and in talks and discussions. The Roman Catholic Church has a fair share of the time available and makes singularly good use of her opportunities. The committee of religious broadcasting effectively blends the contributions of other Churches, and maintains a high standard in the part of the programme for which it is directly responsible. The programme of talks and discussions is on the whole excellent, and its possibilities are being continually explored and developed. The discussions are particularly valuable, and it cannot be denied that non-Christian, not to say anti-Christian ways of thinking are fairly presented, which is as it should be. But there are religious groups and schools of thought, which seldom if ever get the opportunity of being heard on the air. Some exclude themselves and others are excluded against their desire, from co-operation with the main body of Christians through the religious broadcasting committee. The former will include groups of old-style Fundamentalists like the Plymouth Brethren or the Christadelphians. The Christian Scientists also, though not exactly Fundamentalist, are still a self-isolated body. The latter—the groups who would like to co-operate in religious broadcasting but who are at present in practice excluded—may be roughly termed Modernist. The Free-

Christian and Unitarian Churches are among the under-privileged so far as broadcasting facilities are concerned. The Christological issue on which the Free-Christian and Unitarian Churches divide from the great bulk of their fellow-Christians is no doubt so vital that far-reaching co-operation becomes exceedingly difficult. Yet the services of the Socinian movement and its successors to both Christian faith and practice deserve a far more generous appreciation than they have ever yet received from orthodox and evangelical Christians. The record of the major Churches in their dealings with Unitarians is not a happy one. A Pharisaic exclusiveness has too often appeared in the attitude of more orthodox Churches. It would be well if the possibilities of co-operation were examined afresh. But in any case some room should be found in the B.B.C. programme for both the Fundamentalist and the Modernist. One further suggestion may be worth considering. In practice it may be too difficult for the B.B.C. to cater for all religious tastes. But would it not be possible for the B.B.C. on one at least of its stations to sell time, as is done on the American broadcasting corporations? Is not some such concession to private enterprise, to cranks and eccentrics, a desirable qualification to the B.B.C. monopoly? Strict equality of opportunity on the air is unobtainable and probably undesirable, but should not the Christian Church be concerned to secure a closer approximation to it than is realized at present? This may seem a minor matter, but it has some importance for the maintenance of religious liberty.

It remains to consider the special responsibility resting on the Roman Catholic Church at the present time. It is difficult for a Protestant like myself to envisage, still more to trust, the Roman Church as champion of human rights and defender of religious liberty, and yet in the conflict with Nazism and now in taking up the challenge of Marxist Communism, she has cast herself for this particular role. In Germany, the bold utterances of leaders like Cardinal Faulhaber have raised the prestige of the Roman Catholic Church above that of the Confessional Church. It is not surprising that many look to Rome as the protagonist in resistance to totalitarian tyranny, whether Fascist or Communist. For the Roman Church has consistently maintained certain principles which provide guarantees for civil and religious liberty. There is, first, the Catholic conception of Law, which as Troeltsch says 'contrasts sharply with the modern doctrines of the creation of law by the will of the State'. It roots back in the conceptions of *lex naturae* and *jus gentium* to be found in Roman Law. 'Catholic social doctrine conceives Natural Law as existing before the State, which binds it to a positive legal working out of the organic and patriarchal theories of Christian Natural Law.' This means that 'the State, like all positive expressions of law, must order its life according to these principles and that only from this standpoint do its laws attain their binding character'.[1] The Roman Church thus affirms a standard by which State action, the enactment of law and the administration of justice are to be

[1] Troeltsch, *Social Teaching of the Churches*, vol. 1, p. 305.

judged. Law, from this standpoint, is never just the continuation of politics, and must not be degraded to the level of *raisons d'état*. This is the direct contrary to the position taken up by Mr Vyshinsky at the recent Danubian conference.

He was against the proposal to refer disputes to the International Court of Justice and did not agree that politics ended where law began. 'Law', he said,' is an instrument of politics and the reverse theory is untrue.' He did not understand why the Hague Court judges should be thought more impartial than local judges, and suggested that they would merely reflect the views of their own countries.

So long as the Roman Church holds to the reverse theory which Mr Vyshinsky regards as untrue, her claim to be defending liberty is no idle one. This conception of Natural Law has its difficulties, but it does at least oppose a barrier to the claim of the State or of any political party to be a law unto itself. During the Nazi terror, working-class Social Democrats and Confessional Church Christians were drawn together by the common conviction that the State must be subject to law, and that to treat law as the instrument of politics may be convenient to dictators but is essentially immoral. Here genuinely democratic Socialists, Confessional Churchmen and Roman Catholics are at one. The Catholic conception of Natural Law offers a basis on which Catholics can co-operate with others in the defence of civil and religious liberty. The movement known as 'The Sword of the Spirit' has been quick to avail itself of this opportunity.

In the second place, beyond this conception of law, the Roman Catholic Church has consistently declined to subordinate the Church to the State. It has kept clear of Erastianism. Luther accepted too readily the principle *cujus regio, ejus religio*, and indeed in his appeal to the nobility, he did not pay sufficient heed to the Psalmist's warning, 'Put not your trust in princes!' Luther's subservience to the State has been exaggerated in popular estimation of him. Brunner points out that according to Luther's teaching 'there is a right of resistance against tyrannical princes, and even a right to armed resistance....There is no trace of the blind obedience which has always been attributed to Luther.'[1] Nevertheless, Lutherans have not been as independent in judging and, if need be, in opposing the State as have Calvinists and Catholics. The assertion of the independence and supremacy of the Church is itself a safeguard against oppression by the State.

While the Church of Rome is thus defending liberty, civil and religious, against Communist dictatorship, it is severely handicapped in undertaking this defence by being deeply involved in the sin of persecution in the past, by having too readily come to terms with Fascist dictatorships in Italy and Spain, and by its very interpretation of the authority of the Church. It is, to say the least of it, most unfortunate that the history of the Inquisition should provide Bernard Shaw with such an effective line of defence of present-day Communist practice. The persecution to which Catholic bishops

[1] Brunner, *Justice and the Social Order*, p. 237.

and priests are now being subjected and of which the Church rightly complains, is strictly parallel in theory and practice to the persecution to which heretics were subjected by the Inquisition. That the majority of Catholics, at least in the Western democracies, deplore and condemn the cruelties of the Inquisition does not suffice to undo the evil consequences of the long-continued condonation and even justification of such iniquity. It is all to the good that 'in 1816 the Pope authoritatively forbade the further use of torture in all tribunals of the Inquisition: and statements heartily justifying torture, scourging, burning, etc. can now be found only in out-of-date or irresponsible productions'.[1] It is also noteworthy that

when the *Codex Juris Canonici* was officially re-edited in 1917, the only penalties prescribed in it were of a non-temporal character, all penalties not explicitly prescribed (and that includes the death-penalty) were declared to be repealed, and it was laid down that no one was to be compelled to embrace the Catholic faith against his will.[2]

In one of his encyclicals Leo XIII underlined this last consideration. 'The Church is wont to take earnest heed that no one shall be forced to embrace the Catholic faith against his will, for, as St Augustine wisely reminds us, "Man cannot believe otherwise than of his own free will".' It seems then that the Roman Church has definitely disowned the cruelties, the methods of

[1] C. J. Cadoux, *Roman Catholicism and Freedom*, p. 98.
[2] Ibid. p. 52.

inquiry, and the punishments characteristic of the Inquisition. But the principle of restricting heresy and defending orthodoxy by means of the Inquisition and of invoking the aid of the civil power in suppressing error has not been abandoned. Fears of a revival of the use of torture or of a renewal of the fires of Smithfield by governments under Catholic control are, no doubt, groundless, but there is still no security for religious liberty under such governments. As in the U.S.S.R. the concession of religious liberty is a matter of expediency, not of principle in Catholic countries. The Jesuit Father, John Courtney Murray, in a careful review of the middle section of Searle Bates's massive work, *Religious Liberty: an Inquiry*, criticizes it on the ground that it will lend much colour to the assumption, based on faulty philosophical thinking and a superficial reading of history, that active persecution is in the very logic of a religion of dogma and authority.[1] But it is in Catholic quarters that this assumption still prevails, and too many of their theologians are guilty of the faulty philosophical thinking and the superficial reading of history on which it is based. Catholics still interpret the religion of dogma and authority as involving logically the right to persecute. Monsignor Ronald Knox may illustrate the point. In his preface to A. C. Maycock's book on the Inquisition, he defended the medieval plea for religious persecution, by reminding us that 'the faith which is strong enough to make martyrs is strong enough to make persecutors'.

[1] In the Jesuit Review, *Theological Studies* (March 1946), p. 155.

In his own book *The Belief of Catholics*, dated 1927, Monsignor, then Father, Knox wrote:

> You cannot bind over the Catholic Church, as the price of your adhesion to her doctrines, to waive all right of invoking the secular arm in defence of her own principles. The circumstances in which such a possibility could be realized are sufficiently remote.... Given such circumstances, is it certain that the Catholic Government of the nation would have no right to insist on Catholic education being universal (which is a form of coercion) and even to deport or imprison those who unsettle the minds of its subjects with new doctrines? It is 'certain' that the Church would claim that right for the Catholic Government, even if considerations of prudence forbade its exercise in fact.... And for those reasons a body of Catholic patriots, entrusted with the Government of a Catholic State, will not shrink from repressive measures in order to perpetuate the secure domination of Catholic principles among their fellow-countrymen.[1]

Professor Searle Bates cannot fairly be blamed for giving colour and currency to the assumption which Father J. C. Murray deplores. The critic must look for the real culprits nearer home. The position of the Roman Church as the defender of civil and religious liberty against totalitarian encroachments would be immensely strengthened if she would repudiate once and for all the logic which associates the right to persecute with the religion of dogma and authority, if she would once for all surrender the right to invoke the aid of the secular arm in defence of her own principles. It is not enough for Catholic apologists to

[1] Quoted in C. J. Cadoux, op. cit. pp. 59, 60.

point to Catholic States which, as a matter of expediency, practise toleration. The Catholic colony of Maryland was among the first to give constitutional guarantees for freedom of worship. To-day, Catholics point with pride and confidence to the new constitution of Eire, which came into effect on 29 December 1937. Dr Francis J. Connell, in his pamphlet *Freedom of Worship, the Catholic position,* cites the relevant article in full, and on the strength of it claims that 'in practice, Catholic governments are generally much more liberal toward non-Catholics than are distinctively Protestant States towards Catholics'.[1] Article 44 of the Constitution of Eire is indeed admirable, but unfortunately one swallow does not make a summer, and Eire cannot fairly be cited as typical of Catholic governments. We are justified in regarding older established Catholic countries as typical, and their example lends no support to Dr Connell's claim. Spain is more important and more typical than Eire. Anyone who is acquainted with the situation under Franco's régime in Spain will be aware that there is less religious liberty in Spain than there is in the U.S.S.R. A letter contributed to the *Sunday Times* a little while ago understates rather than exaggerates the active persecution to which Protestants and Evangelicals are subjected.

Spain is the only country in Europe, where it is forbidden to print, import or sell a Bible, other than the abbreviated and commented version. The Protestant churches are forced to hold their services

---

[1] Pamphlet, p. 14. The text of Article 44 of the Constitution of Eire is appended in a note at the close of this chapter.

privately and they are open to police supervision.
The Protestant churches are also forbidden to have
any signs as this is regarded as 'propaganda'. Protestants are not allowed to hold public offices. Their
schools have been closed. Protestant marriages are
not recognized by the State. Protestant pastors have
served long years of prison sentences.

So long as this situation continues, it is vain for the
Church to protest against the persecution of Catholics
in Russia and her satellites. The Church lies open to
a devastating and unanswerable *tu quoque* argument.
It is useless for Catholic apologists to say, Why pick
on Spain? Why not look at Eire? The cynical might
say that Eire is on her good behaviour because she
must overcome the distrust and undermine the in-
transigence of Northern Ireland. But without in any
way detracting from the enlightenment and good faith
of the Catholic government in Eire, we still cannot
ignore Spain. In the conflict of religions in the twentieth century, Spain is a strategic centre and Eire is not.
A small advance towards toleration in Spain would be
worth far more than the most generous guarantees of
religious liberty in Eire. It was in Spain that the
Catholic Church first became entangled in the sin of
persecution. Would that the Church had supported
St Martin of Tours in refusing to communicate with
bishops whose hands were stained with the blood of
Priscillianist martyrs! It was in Spain and under
Spanish direction elsewhere, that the Inquisition was
guilty of its worst crimes and excesses. It is in Spain
now that youthful religious fanaticism is encouraged

or at least permitted to express itself in violent attacks on property and persons. It is surely in Spain that some definite repudiation of past errors and some atonement for past sins are most clearly called for from the Catholic Church and its leaders. The sin of persecution began in Spain: it should and must end there. Until there is a radical change in Spanish Catholicism, the Roman Church in opposing Communism will be like a boxer with one hand tied behind his back.

Mr Middleton Murry states the issue clearly in his book *The Free Society*. After describing the peril in which what he calls the Logos-civilization now stands —the peril of being betrayed from within by those blinded intellectuals who are 'working to destroy the twofold conscience and to make the false appear the true and the wrong the right, in the deified lawlessness of the Communist State'—Mr Murry goes on to speak of weaknesses among the defenders of that civilization.

The most powerful of the Christian Churches—the Roman Catholic—has an equivocal record as regards the free society: and though there are now signs of a radical change in its attitude, it is not unreasonable that old and justifiable suspicions of it should persist. After all, the freedom of the twofold conscience had to be established in the teeth of the bitter opposition of the Roman Catholic Church. The wheel has indeed turned full circle: to-day the Roman Catholic Church has its greatest strength in the free society of the United States, because it is a free society. *But not until the Roman Church withdraws its great influence from support of the dictatorship and exerts it for the establishment of a free society in Spain can we be certain that the change of heart and mind is complete.*

Perhaps the greatest obstacle to the change of heart and mind lies in the Catholic conception of Christianity as a religion of dogma and authority. It is temerarious of a heretic to suggest and it may be perilous for the Roman Catholic Church to accept the suggestion that this conception stands in urgent need of revision. But however rash and ill-advised the undertaking, the need of revision is so urgent that the case for it must be elaborated. As popularly presented, the Catholic position combines the principle of doctrinal intolerance with the principle of personal tolerance. There is an inevitable tension between these principles, but as the position now stands the latter principle would forbid a revival of active persecution while the former would justify a Catholic government in restricting religious liberty within the narrowest possible limits. Doctrinal intolerance rests on the belief that

the Catholic Church is the only organization authorized by God to teach religious truth and to conduct public religious worship.... The very existence of any other church is opposed to the command of Christ that all men should join His one Church. From this it follows that, as far as God's law is concerned, no one has a real right to accept any religion save the Catholic religion, or to be a member of any church save the Catholic Church or to practise any form of divine worship save that commanded or sanctioned by the Catholic Church. ... A little thought will show that the Catholic position is perfectly reasonable. Any person who believes in a personal God to whom all creatures are subject must admit that He is entitled to command all men to accept and to practise one particular form of religion. Now, Catholics hold that God has actually done this—that

He has imposed on all men the obligation to accept and to practise Catholicism, the religion founded by the divine Redeemer of the world.[1]

Since then Catholic religion alone is true and all others are false, any government which recognizes any other religion than the Christian religion or any other form of Christianity than the Catholic religion falls into error and sin. It is the duty of the State to recognize, support and defend the one true religion, and to treat any other religion as on equality with Catholic religion, except as a matter of political expediency, is to flout the command of God. 'Doctrinal intolerance signifies nothing else than the logical attitude of mind that any intelligent person takes toward views he knows to be erroneous.'

From this standpoint, Catholic apologists always assume that toleration is the outcome of religious indifference or at least of the uncertainty as to standards of belief which prevail in Protestant and Modernist circles. They tend to agree with Dr Hromadka in regarding the policy of religious freedom and equality as belonging to the era of Liberal bourgeoisie with its indifference, neutrality and tolerant indulgence. And it is certainly difficult to dispute Mill's assertion that the great principle of religious liberty has hardly any-where been practically realized, except where religious indifference has added its weight to the scale. So it seems to the Catholic that toleration as a State policy is part of that Liberalism whose disintegrating tendencies drove Newman to seek refuge in the Roman Church.

[1] F. J. Connell, *Pamphlet on Freedom of Worship*, pp. 4, 5.

Thus the Jesuit Father Murray in his critique of Searle Bates's book, already referred to, says:

A major effort of the whole work is to base religious liberty in religion itself [too simple a Problematik again]. For the out-and-out religious Liberal, who is at least a relativist, if not a complete sceptic in the field of religious truth, this is quite easy. But for the sincere Protestant who still maintains some conception of the absoluteness of religious conviction and the objectivity of religious truth, the task is more difficult. He is continually brought up against what Newman long ago pointed out to be the perennial problem of the Liberal: 'How shall I so maintain that I am right as not to imply that you who contradict me are wrong?' ... The problem is a false one: but the Liberal is none the less stuck with it.[1]

Father Murray assumes that the Liberal's answer to this problem is to recognize relativism in the field of religious truth, and this is taken to be the only way to base religious liberty in religion itself.

The customary answer is in terms of what is called 'humility'. One puts forth one's 'truth' as truth indeed, but with the recognition that the human mind is finite, subject to error, limited in its grasp of truth, and therefore obliged to be, in effect, both categorical and tentative. Not being a Protestant, I quite fail to understand this concept of 'humility' (which is the antithesis, of course of my Roman 'pride'). ... When I say for instance, that there are definitely seven sacraments and definitely not three, I am either correct or mistaken in my assertion. ... To ask me to be properly 'humble' and to assert that there are seven sacraments only in such a way as to leave the door open to the

[1] *Theological Studies*, pp. 160, 161.

possibility that some one else may be quite right in asserting that there are only three, is to ask me to prostitute not only my intelligence but his.[1]

Much might be said in defence of the Protestant or Liberal concept of 'humility' which Father Murray dismisses rather too easily. Cromwell's plea to the Westminster Assembly of Divines—'I beseech you, in the bowels of Christ, think it possible you may be mistaken'—deserves consideration in other quarters. Newman recognized the weight attaching to Bishop Butler's principle that 'probability is the guide of life', and we misuse our intellectual powers when we turn our estimates of probabilities into categorical assertions of absolute truth. That great religious Liberal, Benjamin Jowett, rightly claimed that 'it is a great part of true religion not to say we know more than we do'. To ask a Catholic or any intelligent person for that matter, to hedge when he has clear convictions and must witness to the truth of them is obvious folly. No doubt we cannot contrive to be both categorical and tentative at one and the same time. But if there are some issues on which we should be uncompromisingly dogmatic, there are others on which it is our duty to be tentative. If the Liberal should heed Newman's warning against the Englishman's spirit of compromise which seeks to find a way between right and wrong, truth and falsehood, down the channel of no-meaning, the believer in a religion of dogma and authority needs to beware of defining overmuch. The much-maligned Jesuit theory of probabilism, which

[1] Loc. cit. p. 161.

was in fact dangerous and even disastrous in morals, has a more legitimate application in the sphere of doctrine. Those who are not convinced that the successors of St Peter are exempt from the Apostle's fallibility, may legitimately raise the question whether the Roman Catholic Church in the development of its dogmatic system has not laid on faith unnecessary burdens grievous to be borne. But it is not on such considerations that I would base the plea for a reconsideration of the Catholic conception of authority. Let us assume that God wills all men to be saved through one faith and one Church. Let us assume that the Roman Catholic Church is the one true Church and that God has given her infallible authority to interpret the one true faith. Let us assume that all the dogmas taught by the Church are necessary for the interpretation and defence of the Gospel. It will follow from this that the Church has the right and the duty to define the terms of her communion, to discipline her members and to decide whom to retain and whom to disown. It does not follow that the Church has the right to appeal to the State to aid her in the maintenance of her discipline or in the propagation of her faith. We may go further and say that the doubt as to the claim of the Church to invoke the aid of the State and to encourage the State to set limits to religious liberty is felt more keenly by the sincere Protestant who still maintains some conception of the absoluteness of religious conviction than by the Liberal who has surrendered to relativism and scepticism. For the plea for religious liberty rests not on the Protestant's

uncertainties and hesitations about the dogmas pro-
pounded to interpret and defend the Gospel, but on
his assured conviction as to the nature of the Gospel
itself. The Christian as such is committed to demand
from the State the fullest measure of religious liberty
for others as well as for himself and that not as a matter
of expediency, but on grounds of principle, because
without freedom of worship and freedom of thought
it is impossible to fulfil God's purpose for man in
creation. Furthermore, unless she jealously safeguards
these liberties for all men, the Church cannot fulfil the
ministry of reconciliation which has been entrusted to
her. Religious liberty has its sure foundation, not in
religion itself if by that is meant religion in general,
but in essential Christianity, in the one true religion
which the Catholic Church claims to expound. 'Any
person who believes in a personal God to whom all
creatures are subject must admit that He is entitled to
command all men to accept and to practise one particular form of religion.' No one will hesitate about the
admission, but the Gospel is that God has *not* actually
done this, He has *not* imposed on all men the obligation
to accept and to practise Catholicism. The Gospel is
that the God who, we all admit, is entitled to command,
has in Christ come to invite and to persuade. God
offers salvation to all men, He *pleads* with them to
accept it, He does *not command* them to accept it. Why
is Christ offered to men on the altar daily in every
Catholic Church? To remind them that God has imposed on all men the obligation to accept and to
practise Catholicism, or to commend to them the love

which sent Christ to die for us while we were yet sinners? All this talk of God's law in this connexion is alien from the Gospel itself. Calvary is not an extension of Sinai. This is the ground of the appeal to the Catholic Church to re-think its position. It is not simply a question of the Church taking her rightful place in the struggle for the maintenance of the free society. It is a question of her relation to her Lord. She claims to speak for Christ to men to-day. Can she do so, so long as she sets Law before Gospel, and doctrinal intolerance before personal tolerance? Her primary duty to her Lord and to humanity is to preserve for men the liberty wherewith Christ came to set men free.

Supplementary Note
'Constitution of Eire', Art. 44

The State acknowledges that the homage of public worship is due to Almighty God. It shall hold His name in reverence and shall respect and honour religion. The State recognizes the special position of the Holy Catholic Apostolic and Roman Church as the guardian of the Faith professed by the great majority of the citizens. The State also recognizes the Church of Ireland, the Presbyterian Church in Ireland, the Methodist Church in Ireland, the Religious Society of Friends in Ireland, as well as the Jewish Congregations and the other religious denominations, existing in Ireland at the date of coming into operation of this Constitution. Freedom of conscience and the free profession and practice of religion are, subject to public order and morality, guaranteed to every citizen. The State guarantees not to endow any religion. The State shall not impose any disabilities or make any discrimination on the ground of religious profession, belief or status. Legislation providing State aid for schools shall not discriminate between schools under the management of different denominations, nor be such as to affect prejudicially the right of any child to attend a school receiving public money without attending religious instruction at that school.

CHAPTER VII

RELIGIOUS LIBERTY IN NON-CHRISTIAN COUNTRIES— DANGERS AND SAFEGUARDS

ON 4 December 1946, in the House of Lords, the Archbishop of York, Dr Garbett, initiated a debate on the rights of minorities. He made it clear that he was particularly concerned with the threat to religious liberty and with the position of Christian minorities in Moslem countries.

I take Egypt as an illustration....In that country there are Coptic Churches—the Churches of the people before the Moslem invasion—and there are Greek Orthodox Churches under the Patriarch of Alexandria. There are other ancient Christian Churches and there is active missionary work. When we [the British] occupied Egypt we recognized that these minorities should be protected. When the Montreux agreement was being negotiated, the President of the Egyptian Delegation gave in writing an assurance (which was printed with the agreement) that while the agreement was operative, educational, scientific, medical and charitable institutions of the United Kingdom in Egypt should continue free to carry on their activities. But this convention comes to an end in 1949 and it is doubtful if we can assume that the ancient Churches and the missionary societies in Egypt will continue to possess special religious rights. Most emphatically there is no question of asking for them special privileges—only equal rights with any other citizen in that country....But there have been in recent years

some ominous signs: various attempts have been made
by Egyptian Governments to restrict and to interfere
with the work both of the ancient Churches and of the
missionary societies....Both from a recent visit to
Egypt and from correspondence with responsible
persons there I know that there is great anxiety over
the attitude of the State to Christian minorities when
the Montreux convention ends.[1]

That this anxiety is not groundless is clear from more
recent developments, which are reviewed in the following paragraphs by the Rev. R. D. Rees.

In March 1948, Law No. 38 was passed by the
Government of Egypt regarding private schools. The
purpose of the Law is a desire to bring private schools
within the orbit of State education and to raise their
standards, but some provisions infringe basic rights.
Article 25 of the Law gives the Ministry almost unlimited powers to close any educational institution
without warning. Article 10 discriminates against
schools which have pupils resident in Egypt for a
limited period, by demanding the standard of Arabic
required in Government schools. Article 3 would
make co-education impossible.

Article 11 reads: 'If the private school prepares its
pupils for the public examinations held by the Ministry
of Education it must follow a syllabus which conforms
to that prescribed by the Ministry.' This syllabus
requires the teaching of Islam for Muslim pupils. As
Christian schools prepare their pupils for Government
examinations, this means they must provide instruction in Islam for such pupils. If they are in receipt
of a Government grant, the Ministry is insisting
on the erection of a place for prayer for Muslim pupils
within the school premises.

[1] Hansard, *House of Lords*, vol. 144, No. 10, cols. 595 f.

Article 12 reads: 'No school may teach its pupils, boys or girls (whatever their age), a religion other than their own, even with the consent of the parent.' The Controller of Non-Government Schools has told a deputation that extra curricular activities of a religious character, even if voluntary, come within the terms of this article. If a Christian teacher is asked even out of school by a Muslim pupil concerning the teaching of Christianity on a special point, it would be wiser for the teacher to decline to answer the question. Whatever may be the use in Western countries of a conscience clause, he said that in Egypt the State must protect Muslim children from the abuses of certain schools regarding which many complaints have been received by the Ministry.

This means that the fundamental rights of conscience are violated and the religious education of children is taken out of the hands of parents and monopolized by the State.

It is evident from the provisions of this education act that the Egyptian Government would like to squeeze the private schools out of existence, and will certainly limit Christian education very rigidly. In Egypt, as in other Moslem countries, while Christians and Jews are allowed some freedom of worship for themselves, conversion is resented as apostasy from the true faith and as weakening national unity. Both Arab nationalism and Moslem orthodoxy combine to restrict any form of evangelism or of education which might mislead the faithful. The right to change one's religion is not recognized. The law which affixes the death-penalty to apostasy still holds. Dr Stanley Morrison, whose authoritative survey *Religious Liberty in the Near East* was published this summer by the World Dominion Press, summarized the position in an address to the assembly of the World Council of Churches in Amsterdam. He told the Council that

absence of religious liberty in all Islamic countries has created a conception of citizenship in which neither Christian nor Jew appears to have any legitimate place. He named Egypt, Syria, Irak and Transjordan as particularly guilty of discrimination against non-Moslems. Persia probably accorded the greatest measure of liberty, though recent reports were disturbing.[1]

The countries named form the Arab League, and they are influenced by feelings of Arab nationalism heightened by the advance of Zionism in Palestine. Dr Morrison points out that this conflict naturally imperils the safety of Jewish minorities in these countries. In so far as Christian Churches have supported Zionism, they invite discrimination against Christians as well as against Jews. In Iran and in Turkey, national feeling is not so inflamed as in the Arab League, and civil and religious rights are not so restricted.

The Archbishop of York mentioned that 'there are some who also feel anxiety over the future of Christian minorities in India'. He went on to suggest that legitimate grounds for anxiety exist not so much in the Dominion of India as in some of the independent States in India. He was confident that the new government in India proper will fully respect the civil and religious rights of Christians. Though he did not name

[1] Report in *Birmingham Post*, 28 August 1948.

it, he was less confident about Pakistan and some of
the smaller principalities, Moslem and Hindu, in India.
Here, too, there are some ominous signs, and the very
fact that Pakistan feels itself to be insecure *vis-à-vis*
India tends to bring out the more intolerant spirit in
Islam. We have on the one hand the assurance that
minorities in Pakistan will get a fair deal. Moslems,
we are told, 'have got it in their blood to be not only
fair and just but generous when they are in power'.[1]
But the minorities, whether Sikh or Hindu or Christian,
have no confidence in such assurances. Mr Cantwell
Smith, admittedly a rather unsympathetic witness,
writes:

They have persuaded only themselves of this reputed
magnanimity: other communities have been much
afraid. When, in 1942, the daughter of a prominent
(and nationalist) Muslim chose to marry a non-
Muslim officer in the Indian Air Force, the following
was among the comments appearing in the Pakistani
press: 'If the criminal law of Islam be established, such
sensualists who, for the gratification of their own
carnal appetites, trample on the law of God and
Islamic honour, will be, as a warning to others,
publicly stoned to death and their dead bodies thrown
in the field to feed the kites and crows. But now, when
we are ruled by an infidel government, everybody has
freedom to do and say as he pleases, and our helpless-
ness is so extreme that we cannot even turn out these
hypocrites and vipers from Islam and Muslim society.'[2]

[1] This is not an idle claim. At least in their treatment of Jews,
Moslem powers had a better record than Christians in the
Middle Ages. See the Abridgement of Toynbee's *Study of
History*, p. 138.

[2] W. C. Smith, *Modern Islam in India*, p. 265.

It would be foolish to attach too much importance to the heated language of a journalist in the Orient, but events in Bengal, in Delhi and the Punjab, since India and Pakistan attained Dominion status, make it only too clear that it will be difficult to secure civil and religious rights for Moslems in India and for Hindus in Pakistan, and that the problem is less likely to receive a satisfactory solution in Pakistan than in India. So long as the influence and the memory of Mahatma Gandhi prevail, there will be effective resistance to the bigotry of movements like the Mahasabha in India.

There has recently been published in Holland an important work by Dr J. Verkuyl on *Some aspects of the problem of religious liberty in Asia*.[1] It is a study undertaken in the interests of the work of the Christian Church in Asia. He deals first with Moslem countries where the threat to religious liberty is most serious. But he suggests that Hinduism, while tolerant in the realm of thought and doctrine, is less ready to allow change in social custom and practice. The ideas and customs associated with the caste system of society are antagonistic to religious liberty, and it will long be difficult for the nationalist leaders to live up to the spirit of a resolution adopted at the Delhi Unity Conference in 1924, which laid it down that 'every individual is at liberty to follow any faith and to change it, whenever he so wills'. Even if, as we may hope and expect, legal guarantees of such freedom become part of the constitution of the Dominion of India, the social

[1] Verkuyl, *Enkele Aspecten van het Problem der Gods-deinst-vrijheid in Asie*, p. 87.

pressure of conservative Hinduism will tend to render them nugatory. Gandhi's interpretation of the spirit of Swadeshi will work in the same direction.

Thus [he said] as for religion, in order to satisfy the requirements of the definition [of Swadeshi] I must restrict myself to my ancestral religion....By reason of Swadeshi Spirit, a Hindu refuses to change his religion, not necessarily because he considers it to be the best, but because he can complement it by introducing reforms. Change of heart is perfectly possible in every one of the great faiths.

Gandhi certainly discouraged conversion, though he would never have agreed to penalizing it legally. Dr Verkuyl is inclined to assume that Confucianism, which he suggests turns a sociology into a theology, and ancestor-worship in China present some difficulties for the realization of religious liberty. If there is danger, it emerges in the sphere of education, and though government regulations and controls have created some difficulties in the past and may create more in the future, yet on the whole, the outlook for Christian education in China is a hopeful one. Buddhism, in its orginal form, should be the most tolerant of all religions, but Dr Verkuyl points out that where it has become a State religion, as in Thailand (Siam), Burma and above all in Tibet, the religion of self-denial changes into a religion of tenacious self-assertion. Some monastic groups among Buddhists contrive to combine religious intolerance with power-politics. The development of the situation in Ceylon, at present more hopeful, will be watched with interest. While it cannot be said that any of the great non-Christian religions offer an assured basis for religious liberty, yet it is in Moslem countries that the problem of the maintenance of religious liberty seems most intractable.

The widespread apprehension regarding the present position and future prospects of religious liberty throughout the world lend a special interest to the work of the Economic and Social Council of the United Nations Organization. By Article 68 of the Charter, the Economic and Social Council is directed to 'set up commissions in economic and social fields *and for the promotion of human rights* [italics mine], and such other commissions as may be required for the performance of its functions'. In accordance with this direction, the Council in June 1946 set up a Commission to draw up an International Bill of Human Rights. Eighteen nations are represented on the Commission, including Egypt, India and Iran, the Ukraine, U.S.S.R. and Yugoslavia. The Chairman is Mrs Eleanor Roosevelt. Two years later, the Commission adopted by a majority vote a draft international declaration which will be submitted to the Economic and Social Council at its meeting this year in Geneva. In the first draft declaration, Article 16 defines the provision for religious liberty in three clauses in the following terms:

(1) Every person shall have the right to freedom of religion, conscience and belief, including the right, either alone or in community with other persons of like mind, to hold and manifest any religious or other belief, to change his belief, and to practice any form of

religious worship and observance, and he shall not be required to do any act which is contrary to such worship and observance.

(2) Every person of full age and sound mind shall be free either alone or in community with other persons of like mind to give and receive any form of religious teaching, and in the case of a minor, the parent or guardian shall be free to determine what religious teaching he shall receive.

(3) The above rights and freedoms shall be subject only to such limitations as are prescribed by law and are necessary to protect public order and welfare, morals and the rights and freedoms of others.

This provision for religious liberty is the outcome of two years' deliberation on the part of the Commission, and each step in the discussion and drafting of this declaration has been closely followed by the British Council of Churches, the Conference of British Missionary Societies, and the Joint Committee on Religious Liberty. It is generally recognized that the procedure adopted by U.N.O. is more hopeful than the measures to protect the rights of minorities adopted by the League of Nations. Those measures proved unsatisfactory for two main reasons. Minorities were encouraged to hold themselves aloof from the communities to which they belonged and to look to an outside power to protect them. The obligations contained in the provisions for the protection of the rights of minorities were imposed in peace treaties on particular States, either ex-enemy States or succession States, and this was resented as an infringement of sovereignty that had not been accepted by other

States. The new procedure starts from the rights of individuals rather than of minority groups. It takes the form of an international declaration, and it is hoped this will be followed by a covenant. Endorsement of the declaration and acceptance of the covenant will be by consent in each case and will not be imposed on any State. Moreover, it is a great advantage that the provision for religious liberty should stand part of a general declaration covering human rights of all kinds. The interdependence of civil and religious liberty is so close, that neither can be secured in isolation. In the article on religious liberty, as drafted, special importance attaches to clause 3, which directs that the rights and freedoms claimed in clauses 1 and 2, shall be subject 'only to such limitations as are prescribed by law and are necessary to protect public order and welfare', etc. This clause will fail to attain its object if 'and' is understood to link two distinct and co-ordinated principles. What is intended is that the limitations shall not be left to the arbitrary decision of governments which may then impose any restrictions they please by alleging that these are necessary to protect public order. The suggestion is that the limitations shall be such as are prescribed by positive law, and that such law shall be limited to provisions necessary to protect public order, etc. It will be desirable to make this perfectly clear in the final draft.

While welcoming the draft, the Joint Committee on religious liberty would wish to see it strengthened and clarified in some directions. The Committee notes with regret that a phrase from an earlier draft which claimed freedom 'to Endeavour to Persuade Other Persons of Full Age and Sound Mind of the Truth of his Beliefs' has been dropped from clause 2. It is suggested that the word 'manifest' in clause 1 might be changed to 'communicate' or 'commend', to compensate for the elimination of the word 'persuade' from clause 3. But the article as drafted covers most essentials, and amendments should not be pressed if they would imperil the endorsement by many States of the draft as it stands.

The Joint Committee on Religious Liberty, while heartily approving of the approach to the subject in terms of individual human rights, would yet welcome more explicit reference to the position of minority communities, particularly with reference to the use of their own language in their assemblies, schools and courts. 'In the particular case of community courts, . . . equality of status should apply not only to the status of individuals, but to the status of diverse legal systems and the courts of the different communities.' The Committee would also like Freedom to Maintain Educational Institutions (Schools and Colleges) and Freedom to Own Property for Religious Purposes to be more explicitly stated and more adequately protected. The declaration, however it may be strengthened, will do little to advance human rights unless its main provisions are embodied in a convention or covenant, by which the signatories regard themselves as morally and legally bound. To secure the proper implementation of such a covenant, the Economic and Social Council may need to set up a standing commission. The British Churches favour such developments.

The criticisms and suggestions put forward by the British Churches and outlined in the preceding paragraphs were based on the article as presented to the Commission at Lake Success in June of this year. Article 16 in the draft which the Commission will submit to the Economic and Social Council is shorter and simpler. It runs as follows:

Everyone has the right to freedom of thought, conscience and religion: this right includes freedom to change his religion or belief, and freedom, either alone or in community with others and in public or private, to manifest his religion or belief in teaching, practice, worship and observance.

This formulation of the right to religious liberty is much less adequate than the article with three clauses which it is intended to summarize. At the same time, if adopted, it will go a long way to secure essentials, especially when it is associated with other articles in the proposed declaration of human rights.

The declaration as adopted by the Commission did not secure the support of the Slav group. The Soviet delegate held, apparently, that it leans too much to the Western conception of the relationship between State and individual and does not leave sufficient scope for action by the State to secure the basic economic rights for all its members. The Moslem States, however, are prepared to support the declaration, which will now go forward to the Economic and Social Council. If it is adopted by the Council, it is not likely to reach the Assembly before the autumn of 1949. The declaration, so long as it remains a declaration, 'sets standards to which nations are expected to aspire rather than rules which they may be expected to observe immediately'. Such a declaration if adopted by the Assembly will carry great weight in shaping the policies of nations. If it is followed by a covenant and the covenant is widely accepted, legal sanctions will come into existence which may mark a new epoch in international law. But it would be a mistake to rely too much on action by U.N.O., important as it is. Its importance lies in its being part of a process of education to which the Churches and voluntary organizations must contribute.

Much clearly depends on the relations subsisting between the world's living religions. Dr Verkuyl in his survey of the problem in Asia looks hopefully to Reformist movements in Islam. Such movements are interpreting the duty of *djihad* (Holy War) in a more spiritual way, advocating a return to the way of evangelism rather than the way of military conquest. Similarly in such movements the binding character of the law of apostasy is denied. 'Will Islam succeed in throwing off the yoke of law and tradition and in concentrating upon a few religious principles as its core? Is Lord Cromer's judgement right: "Reformed Islam is Islam no more"? Nobody can foretell.' At the moment Reformism or Modernism in Islam is not advancing, but clearly if ever the tide flows in that direction again, the cause of religious liberty should gain by it.

A movement to promote understanding and fellow-ship among the adherents of the great religions was initiated by the late Sir Francis Younghusband and still continues under the title of the World Congress of Faiths. It is a small uninfluential movement which is having a hard struggle for existence, but it is finely conceived, and if it could secure more adequate support, it would help to undermine bigotry and strengthen faith. For while it is a protest against exclusivism and all forms of religious intolerance, it is not committed to syncretism and the attempt to find the truth of all religion in some highest common factor of living faiths. It is set in the direction indicated in Professor Hocking's Hibbert Lectures on 'the Living Religions and World-faith'. It would persuade adherents of any religion to re-think their religion in the light of a sympathetic understanding of other faiths.[1] In the particular field of the relation between Judaism and Christianity, something effective is being done by the Council of Christians and Jews, which organization has produced an admirable joint pronouncement on the subject of civil and religious rights. If the World Congress of Faiths found more support, we might hope for similar pronouncements from Moslems and Christians, Moslems and Jews, Moslems

[1] Professor Hocking examined three possible ways of arriving at a world-faith. The first he called, 'Radical Displacement'—the substitution of one religion for all others. The second was the way of synthesis, which has all the weaknesses of eclectic philosophies and patchwork quilts. The third he described as the way of reconception, and that is the method which the World Congress of Faiths seeks to follow. A pam-

and Hindus.[1] The value of such pronouncements will lie in the influence on public opinion. But all such movements for mutual understanding are in their infancy, and the initiative for making them effective must come from Christians.

What more can Christians do? It is hardly necessary to reiterate the call for exemplary conduct on the part of governments controlled by Christians. As Canon Guy Rogers insisted, when the draft proposals for an international declaration of human rights were under discussion in the British Council of Churches last spring, 'if we were perfectly honest, we should have to admit that the greatest sinners in the matter were representatives of the Christian religion'. Such honest confession of past failure is certainly called for, and it is equally certain that in some Christian countries a drastic revision of current practice is also necessary. But something more positive than tolerance is required of Christians, a genuine desire to enter into the thought-world of other peoples. If there is a case, as

phlet by Colonel the Rev. J. van Dorp, entitled *Three Temples* and published by the World Congress of Faiths, states the position admirably. The writer takes the Temple at Jerusalem to represent religious exclusiveness, the Temple on Mt Gerizim to stand for religious syncretism, but it is the third Temple, dedicated to worship in spirit and in truth, which each living religion must try to become.

[1] The attention of Moslems might be drawn to the Charter of Protection issued in A.D. 1138 by Muktafi II, Caliph of Baghdad, which was discovered and printed in the *John Rylands Library Bulletin* by Dr Mingana. Sir Mohammed Zafrullah Khan at the United Nations General Assembly, speaking for Pakistan, endorsed article 18 of the Declaration of Human Rights.

Dr Hromadka argues, for active sympathy on the part
of Christians with the aims of the social revolution in
Communist-controlled countries, there is also a case for
active sympathy with national aspirations in countries
like China and India. Just as Christians must refuse to
become the stalking-horse of right-wing economic
and political reaction, so in Asiatic and African lands
they must hold themselves free from every form of
imperialism. As far as possible, the leadership in
evangelism and in church-government should be in
the hands of Christians belonging to the country where
missionaries are at work.[1] But it will also be clear
that the Christian may not secure religious freedom
by unreservedly supporting either Communist programmes or nationalist aims. Nor can the Christian
say simply, 'I approve your aims, though I cannot
approve your methods', since where methods are
inhuman and cruel, there will almost certainly be
something wrong with the aims, however speciously
these aims are represented as embodying the rights and
interests of the people. But it is more important to
consider what Christians can do to promote a sympathetic understanding of other faiths. Already the
comparative study of religions draws most of its
inspiration and owes most of its achievements to
Christian scholars. Has the time come to give a larger
place to this study in Christian education? When the
future of religious instruction in our schools was under
consideration in connexion with the Act of 1944,
a letter appeared in *The Times* over some distinguished

[1] For China, cf. Verkuyl, op. cit. p. 145.

signatures, suggesting that a syllabus embodying the truths and particularly the moral principles common to the great religions would be better than the agreed syllabuses of religious knowledge based on the study of the Bible which are coming into operation throughout the school system. The suggestion did not find favour for many reasons. It was not really in line with the findings either of the comparative study of religions or of child psychology. It assumed too readily the primary importance of the elements which the great religions have in common. It failed to do justice to the special claim which the Bible and the Christian tradition have upon our attention as a people. Moreover the Old Testament, intelligently studied, may be the best introduction to the comparative study of religion and it is not possible for anyone, let alone a child of school age, to appreciate other faiths unless he is first acquainted with the faith that has shaped the culture of the West. Yet the suggestion should not be overlooked. At least in sixth forms and in the young people's colleges there may be found some place for implanting some knowledge of faiths other than the Christian, and in the sphere of adult religious education something still more adequate should be attempted. But if we are right in arguing that in England the first aim of religious education should be to give the child the best understanding of Christianity of which he is capable, can we reject out of hand the suggestion that in Moslem countries the first aim should be a grounding in the tenets of Islam? When I was in Jerusalem some twenty-five years ago, I was told that

Jewish parents were sending their children to Christian schools because the Old Testament was being so well taught there. This may no longer be true, and the Jews and Judaism may be held to constitute a special case, but might not Christian schools in Egypt provide instruction in Islam without waiting to be obliged legally to do so? In discussion and controversy the Christian should seek to be able to state the other man's case better than the other man can state it himself. Might not the Christian educators attempt this, if not in schools then at least in colleges?

It is sometimes suggested that Christians should drop propaganda altogether and trust to the silent witness of life and action. Gandhi seems to have commended such a policy to Christians in India. But Christians cannot give up evangelism. They have a message to deliver, a story to tell to the nations, a gospel that all men need to know and have the right to hear. Without the witness of life and action, such evangelism will be ineffective. But without the spoken word, life and action may lack interpretation, and fail to exert their rightful influence. The circulation and appreciation of the gold of silence are furthered by its exchange with the silver coins of speech. The Church must preach, but she might distinguish more carefully than she sometimes does between evangelism and proselytism. She might remember that her Lord criticized the Pharisees for being over-anxious to make converts. There are ways of persuasion which Christians may not use, forms of bait prohibited to Christ's fishers of men.

The task of preaching the Gospel must be undertaken in great humility. Humility is sometimes supposed to reflect lack of confidence in the message. It is really demanded of the Christian by the nature of the message and his manifest unworthiness to deliver it. The test which the holy and wise anchoret advised the British Bishops to apply in dealing with Augustine of Canterbury was a valid test and other missionaries beside Augustine the Less have failed under it. The passage from Thomas Fuller's *Church History of Britain* is worth transcribing. Fuller digested Bede's narrative into a short dialogue.

BRITISH BISHOPS. Are we to desert our traditions at the preaching of Augustine?

ANCHORET. If he be a man of God, follow him.

BRITISH BISHOPS. But how shall we be able to make trial thereof?

ANCHORET. The Lord saith, 'Take my yoke upon you and learn of me: for I am meek and lowly in heart.' If therefore this Augustine be mild and humble of heart, it is credible that he himself beareth the yoke of Christ and tendereth the same to be borne by you: but if he be cruel and proud it appeareth that he is not of God, neither ought you to heed what he saith.

BRITISH BISHOPS. But how shall we make discovery hereof?

ANCHORET. Contrive it so that he and his may come first into the Synod. And if he rise up when you draw near unto him, hear him obediently, knowing him for a servant of Christ; but if he slighteth you and vouchsafeth not to rise up unto you (seeing you are more in number), let him be slighted by you.[1]

[1] Fuller, *Church History*, 1, 108.

Such humility, the humility which Augustine failed to exhibit, is not the product of uncertainty. It is the outcome and expression of faith.

This is indeed no time for doubt and hesitation. It is a time for a renewal of faith and for rededication to the ministry of reconciliation. If there is to be a new civilization, it must be built on Christian foundations. The coming civilization must be Christian, or it will not come. We shall only be engulfed in a further relapse into barbarism. Justice and freedom can only be secured in the light of two fundamental convictions, first that man though he be a creature and a part of Nature has none the less been created in the image of God, and second that the God who created man in his own image is in Christ reconciling the world to himself. These truths the Christian Church must proclaim in season and out of season. For what Robert Barclay said of agreements for international peace is true also of covenants to protect human rights. In 'An Epistle of Love', Barclay wrote:

Although those Kings and Princes, that are now at Variance, may be by your means brought to lay down Arms and appear to be good Friends and dear Allies, yet unless the Lord Jesus Christ can be Restored to his Kingdom in their Hearts and that Evil Ground of Ambition, Pride and Lust and Vain Glory be removed, that so they may Rule in the Wisdom and Power of God, and not according to their Lusts.... They will kindle the Flame again, and all your Articles will not bind them but they will break them like Straws.... And perhaps if they find it difficult to hit upon any probable Ground or Pretence; if they judge themselves strong enough they will neither trouble themselves nor the World to give a Reason, but tell, that to be at Peace is no longer Consistent with their Glory; and when they have brought about what they have determined, they will let the World know the Reason of it. Hath not manifold Experience proved these things to be true? And seeing it is so, there is, nor can no settled firm established Peace be brought to Christendom, until the Devil's Kingdom be rooted out of Men's Hearts, from which Wars come as the Apostle James testifies; and the Kingdom of Jesus come to be established in the Hearts of Kings and Princes and People, whose Kingdom is a Kingdom of Righteousness and Peace and Joy in the Holy Spirit.[1]

What is true of Peace is true also of Freedom. There is no settled, firm established Freedom except in surrender to Him, whose service is perfect freedom. He must reign.

[1] P. Wragge, *The Faith of Robert Barclay*, pp. 147–8.

HUMAN RIGHTS AND RELIGIOUS FREEDOM

Statement issued by the Joint Committee on Religious Liberty (Great Britain)

I. Religious Freedom and Secular Authority

(1) In Christian belief the essential meaning of all human freedom is freedom to live according to the will of God, which includes the opportunity to exercise and develop in full measure the capacities with which He has endowed human nature, and a corresponding deliverance from conditions which thwart His purpose for mankind.

(2) In the State we recognize an instrument to this end, to be honoured as belonging to a natural order grounded in God's will, and to be wielded with responsibility towards God as the ultimate source and sanction of all authority. The primary functions of the State are to protect its citizens against attack from without and disorder within its own borders; to frame, administer, and uphold a body of law expressive of prevailing conceptions of right; and thus to secure to its citizens freedom from violence and injustice. The due discharge of these high and heavy responsibilities entitles the State to loyalty and obedience from the citizen who enjoys the freedoms thus secured.

Under modern conditions there is a tendency to entrust the State with further general responsibilities for the public good, notably in the fields of education, health, and employment. Believing that freedom from ignorance, freedom from disease, and freedom from want belong to the Divine purpose for men, we recognize that an obligation rests upon the citizen to co-operate loyally with the State in the pursuit of these good ends.

(3) But, in Christian belief, the highest capacity of human nature, and the most important in that its due exercise gives meaning, direction and coherence to all others, is that of knowing, obeying and worshipping God. This capacity for religion is innate in every human being; it can be exercised by the individual in his solitariness at any time and in all circumstances; and it must be thus exercised at certain critical turning-points in personal development. Yet the capacity for religion is essentially also a social capacity requiring for its due development the disciplines and fellowship of a religious community, and demanding expression in appropriate forms of social life.

The freedom proper to religion is therefore two-fold: on the one hand, it consists in the individual's right of direct approach to God, and response to God according to conscience, and of adherence to that religious community which in his private judgement shall best minister to his religious and moral welfare; on the other hand, it consists in the right of a religious community freely to order its own forms of worship and social life for the religious and moral welfare of its members, and to give open witness to the faith which informs its common life.

We claim that such religious freedom is the fundamental human freedom in which alone the true dignity of human personality can be fostered and its highest capacities flower. The right to it is therefore inalienable at all times and in all circumstances, and ought to be acknowledged and duly safeguarded by the State.

But we recognize that this right, while inalienable, is nevertheless in the following sense not an unconditional right: if the adherents to any form of religion so exercise their right of religious freedom as to disturb public order, or endanger public security, or outrage the basic moral conceptions which are essential to both, they do so at their own risk, and the State to which they belong, or in which they are resident, is entitled to invoke the sanctions of law against them. Yet, in the light of history, it must be added that States sometimes unjustifiably curtail religious freedom on an alleged plea of its abuse.

Thus understood and subject to the limit thus indicated, freedom of religion is not a special privilege claimed for minority groups, but rather a universal human right. As such, it ought to be embodied in any International Bill of Rights which may be framed, and to be under-written by all the signatories.

II. A CHARTER OF RELIGIOUS FREEDOM

When analysed more closely and reduced to terms of particular civil rights, religious freedom will be found to require safeguards at least as comprehensive and as specific as those contained in a charter such as the following:

(1) Freedom of religion is an essential and integral aspect of human freedom. It includes the freedom of all human beings to choose for themselves their religious belief and adherence, and to change them if they so desire.

(2) The rights which guarantee the full development of human beings, in the integrity and dignity of their human personality, include the religious rights not only of freedom to worship according to conscience, but also of freedom to educate, to propagate and to persuade, and to conduct social and charitable activities.

(3) The rights of meeting guaranteed by a community to its members include the right of

meeting for the purpose of worship according to conscience.

(4) The rights of association guaranteed by a community to its members include the right of association for religious purposes—that is to say, not only for the purpose of worship according to conscience, but also for the purposes of religious education, propagation and persuasion, and of social and charitable activities. Religious associations are accordingly free, on the same basis as other associations and subject to the same limits imposed by the necessities of public order, security and morality, to acquire and hold property, and to act generally for the fulfilment of their purposes.

(5) The rights of freedom of expression of thought (by speech, writing, printing and publishing) guaranteed by a community to its members include the rights of expression of religious thought, of the propagation of religious belief, and of religious persuasion, subject to the same limits as are imposed on the general freedom of expression of thought by the necessities of public order, security and morality.

(6) The rights of children to receive instruction and education with a due regard to their freedom include the right to receive religious instruction and education when such instruction and education is desired by their parents.

(7) The rights of religious freedom—in meeting for worship, in association, in the expression of thought, and in instruction, education, and persuasion—include the right of persons and groups to be guaranteed against legal provisions and administrative acts which are calculated to impose disabilities on grounds of religion.

III. EXPLICATION OF CERTAIN POINTS IN THE CHARTER

The experience of the Committee, gathered from many parts of the world, puts it beyond doubt that, if religious freedom is to be materially effective, the last provision in the Charter given above requires considerable elaboration, especially as it affects the provisions contained in the first, fourth and sixth paragraphs.

(1) *The individual's right to choose or change his religious belief and adherence* will not be materially effective if by reason of its exercise he should:

(*a*) lose complete and full protection of life and liberty;

(*b*) forfeit equality before the law in respect of any civil or political right;

(*c*) be deemed to be under a legal incapacity to take any share in a succession to property or to take under a will.

(2) *The right of association for religious purposes* will be materially ineffective if it omits any one of the following specific rights of religious communities:

(*a*) to be recognized as legal corporations;

(*b*) to appoint without hindrance their own leaders and officers;

(*c*) to train their leaders and workers in theological institutions, and in other ways;

(*d*) to erect, repair and lease buildings for worship and for educational, social and charitable purposes, to open and maintain institutions for such purposes, and to appoint their own staff in them, provided their qualifications conform to the minimum technical standards required by the State in such institutions;

(*e*) to maintain, in religious, educational, social and charitable activities, free connexion with their co-religionists in other countries, and to receive from other countries contributions towards such activities without deduction;

(*f*) to enjoy, without discrimination, all privileges which are given to any religion in respect of taxation, customs dues, the ownership, sale and transfer of property, etc.

(3) *The right of religious instruction and education* will be materially ineffective if it is not safeguarded by the following specific provisions:

(*a*) no minor shall be taught a religion other than that of his parents or guardians without their consent;

(*b*) in any State which contains substantial religious minorities and in which religious instruction is given in the State schools, there shall be opportunity for the minority communities to provide special religious teaching for their own children;

(*c*) all citizens shall have the right, whether individually or in association with others, to open schools and other educational institutions for members of their own religious communities and for others in which:

(i) they may teach their own religion freely, subject to a conscience clause in the case of members of other faiths;

(ii) they are free from the obligation to teach any religion, *qua* religion, other than their own;

(iii) they may appoint their own staff in all subjects, provided their scholastic qualifications are adequate;

(iv) if the schools are unaided, they may follow their own curricula and their own methods

of instruction, provided these do not contra-
vene Government requirements regarding
health and sanitation, financial administration and technical efficiency;

(v) they may participate in Government grants
to non-government schools without discrimination on religious grounds;

(vi) their students are admitted without discrimination to Government examinations.

IV. The Problem of Religious Minorities

(1) Religious freedom is a matter of groups as well
as of individuals; indeed it is perhaps even more
a matter of groups than of individuals. As a matter of
groups, it raises—and has always raised in the course
of history—the problem of religious minorities. The
dominant religious group of a territory or state, con-
fronted by other and smaller groups, has often felt
impelled either to demand conformity or to impose
disabilities. That impulse partly proceeds from an
instinct, common to all groups, directed to the establishment of what may be called a common pattern;
but the instinct is reinforced, and may even seem to be
sublimated, when a religious group has the additional
sense of being a custodian of truth, and feels itself
moved by the motive of making the truth prevail.
Nor are group-instincts and the sense of a special
custodianship of truth the only factors. Motives
and impulses are generally mixed in the tangle of
human affairs; and an issue which at first sight may
seem to be purely a religious issue will often be found,
on further inquiry, to be complicated by other factors.
Religious feeling, consciously or unconsciously, may
be mixed with nationalism; and it may similarly be
mixed with racialism. A nation, for example, in which
the predominant religious group is Mohammedan

may feel that Mohammedanism is the core of its
nationality; and if such a nation should also cherish
the sense of a racial kinship with other nations in
which the predominant religious group is equally
Mohammedan, it may proceed to feel that Mohammedanism is not only the core of its own nationality,
but also the core of a general racial unity which draws
the kindred nations together. The problem of religious
minorities may thus be something more than a problem of religion.

(2) In the course of history three stages or methods
may be traced in the handling of the problem of
religious minorities.

The first stage or method is one which remits the
handling of the problem to the internal jurisdiction of
each State. In England, for example, there was a long
struggle between the Established Church and the
Dissenting Churches; and that struggle formed a great
issue of English domestic politics. Gradually the
demand for conformity and the imposition of disabilities were abandoned; but the process took more
than two centuries. Eventually, however, by a process
of domestic settlement, the problem may be said to
have reached a solution; and the assurance of complete
freedom and equality before the law did justice, and
brought contentment to English religious minorities.
The question may naturally be raised why the problems
of religious minorities should not similarly be treated
as a matter of internal jurisdiction in *all* States. The
answer may perhaps be found in a brief review of the
actual exercise of such jurisdiction during the course
of modern history. Such a review suggests that the
English precedent, if it be a precedent, does not afford
a basis of general policy. Internal jurisdiction has too
often resulted in measures which are repugnant to the
general conscience of men. Sometimes religious
minorities have been simply expelled: sometimes an

attempt has been made, short of this extreme policy, to effect an interchange of minorities; but in either case minorities so treated have been torn up from their roots in the soil and deprived of old social attachments. Sometimes, again, minorities have been retained; but the retained minorities have been either subjected to measures intended to absorb them by force into the life of the majority group, or condemned to live a life of segregation on an inferior level of citizenship and rights, with various disabilities—political, civil, social and economic. Not that these policies of expulsion, or compulsory absorption, or enforced segregation, have been generally or uniformly pursued. States have varied in their attitudes to religious minorities; and if some States have followed these policies, others—alike in the East and West—have followed a policy of justice, and of the freedom and equality of all religious confessions. In the same way as States have varied in their attitude to minorities, minorities also have varied in their attitude to the State. Some have shown loyalty to the States in which they were contained, and a readiness to co-operate with their authorities: others, looking to larger bodies of co-religionists in other States, and with a mixture of motives which might include secular factors of nationality or race as well as the motive of religion, have been intransigent. There are minorities which are apt to think in terms of their rights, and to forget the corresponding duties.

(3) In this position, and under these conditions, a second method of handling the problem of religious minorities emerged. This is a method of international action which takes the form of stipulations contained in treaties. A number of causes led to the adoption of this form of international action. Under modern conditions of communication and commerce, which bring all States into closer contact, a problem of religious

minorities in one State may present itself clearly and vividly to their co-religionists in other States: it may affect, and even embitter, international relations. Again, and on a higher level, there may also be traced —not only in the present century, but also in the nineteenth—the growth of a general public opinion, common to many States, which deprecates, and may even resent, injustices and inequalities (or what it regards as such) inflicted upon minorities in contravention of its own standards. Under the influence of such causes the principle began to be asserted that the relations between States and minorities (among them religious minorities) cannot be left entirely to the internal jurisdiction of all the States concerned. This principle (which had already been at work in the nineteenth century) was adopted in some of the treaties concluded after the war of 1914–18. In these treaties, and also in the mandates formulated under the Covenant of the League of Nations, specific provisions were incorporated for the protection of minorities; and it was stipulated, in some cases, that issues raised by the treatment of minorities were matters of international concern affecting the League of Nations.

The purpose of these provisions was to ensure (i) that the States affected by them should recognize the rights of minorities in their constitution and laws, and (ii) that their courts and administrative officials should give actual and practical effect to such constitutional and legal recognition. The second of these purposes was no less important than the first. Much was bound to depend on the action of courts and administrative officials in the actual interpretation and the practical enforcement of constitutional and legal provisions. If they took their duties seriously, they would make the safeguards for the liberty and equality of religious minorities effective and valuable. If, on the other hand, they gave a large latitude to considerations of 'public order', and brought such considerations largely to bear on their treatment of religious minorities, they might render the safeguards for these minorities contained in constitutional and legal provisions comparatively ineffective.

In any case, and even if this difficulty is surmounted, the handling of the problem of religious minorities by the method of international action which takes the form of stipulations contained in treaties presents other difficulties. A State bound by such stipulations may resent them, as an infringement of its 'national sovereignty'—especially when it sees them peculiarly and (as it thinks) invidiously imposed on itself, while many other States are free from any such obligation. Again the handling of the problem of religious minorities by the method of treaty brings it into the sphere of diplomacy, and may thus subject it to the considerations of national interest and national policy, which inevitably play their part in the conduct of diplomacy. It would thus appear that something further than international action proceeding through treaty stipulations is necessary. Such action is indeed an advance on the unfettered action of the internal jurisdiction of States. But it seems to invite and demand a still further advance.

(4) A third method of handling the problem of religious minorities is now beginning to emerge in the thought and discussion of to-day; and this is the method which invites and demands exploration. Briefly it is the method of making a just treatment for religious minorities incumbent on all States alike, without any particular and possibly invidious reference to particular States. This would involve, as a speaker in the British Parliament has recently suggested, some general declaration by all the United Nations; some general statement of a standard to which all the members of the United Nations would be expected, and

would expect one another, to conform: and, in the last resort, some application of sanctions by the collective authority of the United Nations in the event of failure to conform. This would be a method of international action which was fully and entirely international; and it would transcend the method of international action which takes the form of stipulations in treaties binding only on particular States. The best hope may thus be argued to be, as the Archbishop of York recently stated in Parliament, 'to find a place in the proposed Charter or Bill of Human Rights for a declaration insisting on civil and religious freedom for individuals and minorities'. Whether or no any sanction were added, such a declaration, proceeding from the whole body of the United Nations, would be a new milestone of advance. It would be a Magna Carta of the rights of religious minorities; and it might well be the case that if breaches of that Magna Carta were reported to and ventilated in the meetings of the United Nations, such report and ventilation would themselves be sufficient sanction.

The conclusion of the whole matter would thus seem to be this—that the British public should strengthen the hands of its government, and urge it to associate with other governments, in pressing for the formulation of a Declaration of Human Rights to which all States would be invited to become signatories. Such a Declaration should include, as one of its cardinal articles, the rights of religious minorities to profess and practise their faith freely, on terms of equality with religious majorities, with no disabilities (whether political, legal, social or economic), and with a full recognition of all the safeguards proposed in sections II and III above.

It only remains to add that in urging the need of a Declaration of the Human Rights which it believes should be secured to all religious groups in all States,

the Joint Committee on Religious Liberty is concerned
not with privileges claimed for any particular religious
minority (Christian, Mohammedan, Jewish, or other),
but with the creation of a general standard, and the
formulation of general principles of action. It would
deprecate, and deprecate strongly, the conducting
and carrying on of political or other non-religious
activities by any religious minority on the plea of
religious rights, as it would equally deprecate any
curtailing of the religious rights of such a minority
under the plea and on the ground of public order,
which must indeed always be maintained, but should
never be made a plea for curtailing the genuine exercise
of religious rights by any religious group.

THE UNIVERSAL
DECLARATION OF HUMAN RIGHTS

As approved by The United Nations Assembly
at Paris on 10 December 1948.

[Only the preamble and those of the articles which bear most immediately on the issue of religious liberty are printed here.]

Preamble

Whereas recognition of the inherent dignity and of the equal and inalienable rights of all members of the human family is the foundation of freedom, justice and peace in the world,

Whereas disregard and contempt for human rights have resulted in barbarous acts which have outraged the conscience of mankind and the advent of a world in which human beings shall enjoy freedom of speech and belief and freedom from fear and want has been proclaimed as the highest aspiration of the common people,

Whereas it is essential, if man is not to be compelled to have recourse, as a last resort, to rebellion against tyranny and oppression, that human rights should be protected by the rule of law,

Whereas the peoples of the United Nations have in the Charter re-affirmed their faith in fundamental human rights, in the dignity and worth of the human person and in the equal rights of men and women and have determined to promote social progress and better standards of life in larger freedom,

WHEREAS Member States have pledged themselves to achieve, in co-operation with the United Nations, the promotion of universal respect for and observance of human rights and fundamental freedoms,

WHEREAS a common understanding of these rights and freedoms is of the greatest importance for the full realization of this pledge,

Now therefore the General Assembly

PROCLAIMS this Universal Declaration of Human Rights as a common standard of achievement for all peoples and all nations, to the end that every individual and every organ of society, keeping this Declaration constantly in mind, shall strive by teaching and education to promote respect for these rights and freedoms and by progressive measures, national and international, to secure their universal and effective recognition and observance, both among the peoples of Member States themselves and among the peoples of territories under their jurisdiction.

Article 1

All human beings are born free and equal in dignity and rights. They are endowed with reason and conscience, and should act towards one another in a spirit of brotherhood.

Article 2

1. Everyone is entitled to all the rights and freedoms set forth in this Declaration, without distinction of any kind, such as race, colour, sex, language, religion, political or other opinion, national or social origin, property, birth or other status.

2. Furthermore no distinction shall be made on the basis of the political, jurisdictional or inter-

national status of the country or territory to which a person belongs, whether this territory be an independent, Trust, Non-Self-Governing territory, or under any other limitation of sovereignty.

Article 10

Everyone is entitled in full equality to a fair and public hearing by an independent and impartial tribunal, in the determination of his rights and obligations and of any criminal charge against him.

Article 11

1. Everyone charged with a penal offence has the right to be presumed innocent until proved guilty according to law in a public trial at which he has had all the guarantees necessary for his defence.

2. No one shall be held guilty of any penal offence on account of any act or omission which did not constitute a penal offence, under national or international law, at the time when it was committed. Nor shall a heavier penalty be imposed than the one that was applicable at the time the penal offence was committed.

Article 12

No one shall be subjected to arbitrary interference with his privacy, family, home or correspondence, nor to attacks upon his honour and reputation. Everyone has the right to the protection of the law against such interference or attacks.

Article 13

1. Everyone has the right to freedom of movement and residence within the borders of each state.

2. Everyone has the right to leave any country, including his own, and to return to his country.

Article 14

1. Everyone has the right to seek and to enjoy in other countries asylum from persecution.

2. This right may not be invoked in the case of prosecutions genuinely arising from non-political crimes or from acts contrary to the purposes and principles of the United Nations.

Article 16

1. Men and women of full age without any limitation due to race, nationality or religion, have the right to marry and to found a family. They are entitled to equal rights as to marriage, during marriage and at its dissolution.

2. Marriage shall be entered into only with the full consent of both intending spouses.

3. The family is the natural and fundamental group unit of society and is entitled to protection by society and the State.

Article 18

Everyone has the right to freedom of thought, conscience and religion; this right includes freedom to change his religion or belief, and freedom, either alone or in community with others and in public or private, to manifest his religion or belief in teaching, practice, worship and observance.

Article 19

Everyone has the right to freedom of opinion and expression; this right includes freedom to hold opinions without interference and to seek, receive and impart information and ideas through any media and regardless of frontiers.

Article 20

1. Everyone has the right to freedom of assembly and association.

2. No one may be compelled to belong to an association.

Article 26

1. Everyone has the right to education. Education shall be free, at least in the elementary and fundamental stages. Elementary education shall be compulsory. Technical and professional education shall be made generally available and higher education shall be equally accessible to all on the basis of merit.

2. Education shall be directed to the full development of the human personality, and to the strengthening of respect for human rights and fundamental freedoms. It shall promote understanding, tolerance and friendship among all nations, racial or religious groups, and shall further the activities of the United Nations for the maintenance of peace.

3. Parents have a prior right to choose the kind of education that shall be given to their children.

Article 27

1. Everyone has the right freely to participate in the cultural life of the community, to enjoy the arts and to share in scientific advancement and its benefits.

2. Everyone has the right to the protection of the moral and material interests resulting from any scientific, literary or artistic production of which he is the author.

Article 29

1. Everyone has duties to the community in which alone the free and full development of his personality is possible.

2. In the exercise of his rights and freedoms, everyone shall be subject only to such limitations as are determined by law solely for the purpose of securing due recognition and respect for the rights and freedoms of others and of meeting the just requirements of morality, public order and the general welfare in a democratic society.

3. These rights and freedoms may in no case be exercised contrary to the purposes and principles of the United Nations.